Making and Breaking the Grid

A Graphic Design Layout Workshop

GLOUCESTER MASSACHUSETTS

Making and Breaking the Grid

ROCKPORT PUBLISHERS

Written, compiled, and designed by

Timothy Samara

Understanding structure and freedom in design,

© 2002 by Rockport Publishers, Inc.
First paperback edition published 2005
All rights reserved.
No part of this book may be reproduced in any form
without written permission of the copyright owners.
All images in this book have been reproduced with the
knowledge and prior consent of the artists concerned,
and no responsibility is accepted by producer, publisher,
or printer for any infringement of copyright or otherwise,
arising from the contents of this publication. Every effort
has been made to ensure that credits accurately comply
with information supplied.

First paperback published in the
United States of America by
Rockport Publishers, Inc.
33 Commercial Street
Gloucester, MA 01930-5089
978.282.9590
978.283.2742 fax
www.rockpub.com

Library of Congress Cataloging-in-Publication Data available

ISBN 1-59253-125-3
10 9 8 7 6 5 4 3

Cover and text design **Timothy Samara**

Printed in China

from theory
into real-world
application

A Graphic Design Layout Workshop

Thoughts on Structure:
An Introduction

**For some
graphic designers,
it has become
an unquestioned
part of the
working process
that yields
precision, order,
and clarity.**

**For others,
it is symbolic of
Old Guard
aesthetic oppression,
a stifling cage
that hinders
the search for
expression.**

The typographic grid is an organizing principle in graphic design whose influence is simultaneously ingrained in current practice and fought over in design education, revered and reviled for the absolutes inherent in its conception.

It is a principle with roots in the oldest societies on the planet. Eking out an existence with some kind of meaning—and creating an understandable order for that meaning—is one of the activities that distinguishes our species from all others. Structural thinking, even before its latest codification through European and American Modernism, has been a hallmark of cultures struggling toward civilization. The Chinese, the Japanese, the Greeks and Romans, the Inca—all of these cultures have pursued structural ideas in laying out their towns, conducting warfare, and arranging images. In many instances, that structure was predicated on the notion of intersecting axes that corresponded to the intersection of sky and earth.

The grid instituted by Modernism restated that long-ingrained sense of order, formalizing it yet another degree and transforming it into an established part of design. The typographic grid—a fundamental tenet of the International Style—is an orthogonal planning system that parcels information into manageable chunks. The assumption of this system is that placement and scale relationships between informational elements—whether words or images—help an audience understand their meaning. Like items are arranged in similar ways so that their similarities are made more apparent and, therefore, more recognizable. The grid renders the elements it controls into a neutral spatial field of regularity that permits accessibility—viewers know where to locate information they seek because the junctures of horizontal and vertical divisions act as signposts for locating that information. The system helps the viewer understand its use. In one sense, the grid is like a visual filing cabinet.

For the graphic designers who helped society struggle to move forward after two unimaginable wars, order and clarity became their most important goals. Part of that order, of course, meant consumer comforts; and the businesses that provided them recognized soon enough that the grid could help organize their image, their corporate culture, and their bottom lines.

As the use of grids has changed from self-conscious gesture to that of second-nature reflex, so, too, has the viewing public become more accustomed to information presented to them in greater quantities, simultaneously, in greater complexity, and in more languages. And they're not simply accustomed to it: they want it that way. The grid's minimal simplicity is somewhat at odds with the kinetic, shifting surface of multimedia; information isn't flat anymore, and the average person expects it to move, jump, twist, and make noise. Paradoxically, the corporations that clothed themselves in the grid's neutral, utopian uniform helped create the oversaturated environment that is currently in demand.

As an institutionalized metaphor for all that is right in the world—the intersection of heaven and earth made manifest in every object it governs—the grid has also been imbued with an explicitly spiritual quality. Its early proponents among the European avant-garde fought zealously on its behalf: Theo van Doesburg's mere tilting of the 90° de Stijl axis caused his partner, Piet Mondrian, to sever ties; Josef Müller-Brockmann, the grid's Swiss champion in the 1950s and 1960s, defined its will to order in nearly canonical terms.

Recent years have seen the design profession come to the forefront of public consciousness as our culture reacts to new communications technology. In the information age, it's become an especially important discipline. Within the design community, discussions of accessibility, gender, race, and other social concerns are given greater priority than simple conversations about form and organization; it's hard to find that kind of discussion in the design industry any more. Given that form making and its organization are inextricably linked to the visual dissemination of information, however, it seems likely that this simple discussion could really be a bit more complex, perhaps even wrapping these same "bigger issues" that graphic designers have been giving more attention … an aesthetic 'unconscious' of sorts we've decided to ignore without realizing its fundamental hegemony.

The current era is a little bit like that of Victorian England during the first Industrial Revolution, in the sense that we're living through

another paradigmatic shift in technology and culture:

Our appliances talk to us, our vision is global. The world's vast space has been reduced metaphorically as well as physically, and we're learning to cope with an uncomfortable intimacy as the private self recedes and resources dwindle. Our own industrial revolution's similarity to its antecedent continues, not unexpectedly, in its influence on the arts. A plurality of oft conflicting approaches in architecture, painting, filmmaking, and design reflects the general cultural confusion that pervades the beginning of this millennium.

Amid discussions of race and gender, conservation, political empowerment, and civil rights, perhaps a simple conversation about where to put things—the 'mundane housekeeping' of grid-based design— might have value again.

In the context of our new era of evaluating the course of the design profession on a smaller scale and of the culture at large, the unifying principle of the grid—as well as the value of other kinds of organizational ideas—is a topic that bears renewed consideration as a focus for discussion.

Although it's a start, this book is by no means a theoretical treatise aimed at opening that discussion; it's simply an overview of the subject of visual organization in graphic design. It can be valuable in different ways depending on the reader's background. Designers who haven't formally been introduced to grid use, or who usually avoid using them, may find inspiration to pursue new methods; designers who always use grids may reevaluate the organizing potential of more organic or spontaneous structures. To students, this book can be a valuable resource for seeing a diversity of related work in context, as well as a companion to the formal studies they may be undertaking.

The first section of this book, **Making the Grid,** exposes the reader to the grid's development as an organizing principle and shows it in action. A historical essay and relevant works, arranged chronologically, help the reader trace the evolution of structurally oriented design. **Grid Basics** leads the reader through the essential mechanics of grid building, and the remainder of the section shows examples of completed projects whose design is inherently grid based.

The second section, **Breaking the Grid,** explores the alternatives: deconstruction of grid-based layouts, spontaneous composition, and organic organizational methods. Designers and students will learn how these layout approaches developed historically in tandem with structural methods. The majority of the second section shows contemporary design work that successfully violates the grid or ignores it altogether.

The project exhibits are each given a full spread for thorough exposition and their structures are simply diagrammed. Furthermore, projects with related structures, whether grid-based or not, are notated for comparison so that the reader can understand their similarities and differences more easily. A key at the beginning of each exhibit section clarifies the notation.

Overall, designers and students will benefit from seeing a wide range of exemplary real-world projects that take theory into practice.

1

Making the C

Grid

The history of the grid's development is convoluted and complex. Modern graphic design, as we know it, is a young profession, but incidences of grid use predate the Romans and the Greeks; a full exposition of that history would be impossible here. For our purposes, the grid that is used in Western graphic design evolved during the Industrial Revolution. Ideas circulate in artistic communities, however; trying to pinpoint the precise genesis of one does history a disservice. Gathered here is a rather simplified overview of a complicated process. Contributions by thousands of designers, over more than a century, have been generalized into a few pages; many have been overlooked or mentioned only briefly in passing. The bibliography at the end of this book will help interested readers pursue a more in-depth understanding of this intricate subject.

Coming to Order
A Brief History of the Grid
in Modern Graphic Design

The Brave New World of Industry The grid's development over the past 150 years coincides with dramatic technological and social changes in Western civilization and the response of philosophers, artists, and designers to those changes. The Industrial Revolution that began in 1740s England changed the way people lived—its effect on our culture was fundamental. As the invention of mechanical power induced people to seek a living in cities, power shifted away from the land-owning aristocracy toward manufacturers, merchants, and the working class. Demand from an urban population with ever-increasing buying power stimulated technology, which, in turn, fueled mass production, lowered costs, and increased availability. Design assumed an important role in communicating the desirability of material goods. In addition, the French and American revolutions facilitated progress in social equality, public education, and literacy and helped to create a greater audience for reading material.

With this enormous psychographic change came aesthetic confusion. The Beaux-Arts tradition, much unchanged since the Renaissance and bolstered by the strong moral and spiritual convictions of the times, held on to its aesthetic contrivances and notions of neoclassical taste. A Victorian penchant for Gothic architecture merged oddly with exotic textures imported from the outreaches of the British Empire.

Contradictory design approaches and the need to supply the consuming masses with products reached a kind of plateau in 1856 when writer and designer Owen Jones produced *The Grammar of Ornament,* an enormous catalog of patterns, styles, and embellishments that were co-opted to mass-produce poorly made goods of questionable aesthetic quality.

Fitness of Purpose   The English Arts and Crafts movement in architecture, painting, and design grew out of a reaction to this decline. At the movement's forefront was William Morris, a young student of privileged background who had become interested in poetry and architecture—and their seeming disconnection with the industrialized world. Morris was inspired by John Ruskin, a writer who insisted art could be the basis of a social order that improved lives by unifying it with labor, as it had in the Middle Ages. Together with Edward Burne-Jones, a fellow poet and painter, and Philip Webb, an architect, Morris undertook the revitalization of England's daily aesthetic life. Webb's design of Red House in 1860 for a just-married Morris organized the spaces asymmetrically, based on their intended uses, thereby dictating the shape of the facade. At the time, this idea was unheard of—the prevailing neoclassical model called for a box layout with a symmetrical facade.

Furthermore, no suitable furnishings existed for such a house. Morris was compelled to design and supervise the production of all its furniture, textiles, glass, and objects, becoming a master craftsman in the process. The company that resulted from this experience, Morris and Company, vigorously advocated the notion that fitness of purpose inspired form; their prolific output in textiles, objects, glass, and furnishings heralded a way of working that responded to content, was socially concerned, and paid utmost attention to the finished quality of the work, even when it was mass-produced.

Arthur Mackmurdo and Sir Emery Walker, two of Morris' contemporaries, directed his attention toward type and book design. Mackmurdo's periodical, *The Hobby Horse,* espoused the same qualities—a purposeful proportioning of space and careful control of type size, type selection, margins, and print quality—to which Morris had aspired, but in printed form. In 1891, Morris established the Kelmscott Press in Hammersmith, producing exquisitely designed books in which the typefaces, woodblock illustrations, and materials were designed for their aesthetic integration and ease of production. Morris's most ambitious project was *The Works of Geoffrey Chaucer,* produced in 1894. Its illustrations, display type blocks, and carved initials were integrated through size relationships, and its layouts conformed to an overall predetermined structure that dramatically unified the pages and allowed for faster production. This book signaled a transition from medieval block manuscript (which paradoxically provides its aesthetic framework) to modern page layout, where multiple types of information are integrated into an articulated space.

The Arts and Crafts style gained momentum and was transformed in a number of ways— evolving into the sensuously organic style known as Art Nouveau in France; as the painterly, more architectural Jugendstil in Germany and Belgium—as designers became accustomed to the effects of industrialization. They sought new forms of expression that would speak to the inventive spirit of the age.

The Architecture of Space   Influenced by a trip to England, the work of American architect Frank Lloyd Wright began a systematic evolution away from the organic while continuing to embody the same Arts and Crafts ideals. Like Philip Webb, Wright's work expressed a view that space was the essence of design, in which "the part is to the whole as the whole is to the part, and which is all devoted to a purpose." Proportional relationships, rectangular zones, and asymmetrical organization became guiding principles of what was becoming Modernism. A group of Scottish collaborators—two sisters, Frances and Margaret McDonald, and their husbands, James MacNair and Charles Rennie Macintosh, who had met as students at the Glasgow School of Art—translated the medieval

flair of Arts and Crafts into more abstract and geometric articulations of space. They became known as the Glasgow Four, and publication of their work in book arts, objects, and furniture design in the periodical *The Studio* popularized their ideas as far away as Vienna, Austria and Hamburg, Germany.

An Expanding Influence   Peter Behrens, an aspiring young German architect, grew up in Hamburg under this new influence, as well as that of the Viennese Secession, a countermovement that drew its inspiration from the Glasgow Four and Wright. The Secession distinguished itself with even more rectilinear approaches to poster and book design, as well as architecture. Designers and architects like Josef Hoffman, Koloman Moser, and Josef Maria Olbrich pursued functional simplicity and eschewed decoration. In 1900, Peter Behrens moved to an artists' colony in Darmstadt, established by the Grand Duke of Hesse. One of the other seven artists invited by the Grand Duke and given land to build a house was Josef Maria Olbrich. Through the effort of designing his house and all of its contents, Behrens—like Morris, and in close aesthetic alignment with Olbrich—found himself caught up in the same rational movement that sought order and unity among the arts. Along with industrial design and furniture, he also began to experiment with book layout and the new sans serif typefaces that were beginning to appear from foundries like Berthold. His first book, *Celebration of Life and Art,* is believed to be the first running text set in a sans serif face. Although this book maintains a block-manuscript approach to the composition of the page, it follows in the footsteps of Morris's spatially conceived works of Chaucer and lays important groundwork for grid development in its use of sans serif type. The more uniform texture of sans serif letterforms creates a neutrality within text that emphasizes its shape against the surrounding white space; placement and interval assume greater visual importance.

Behrens moved to Düsseldorf in 1903 to direct that city's School of Arts and Crafts, developing preparatory curricula that focused on fundamental visual principals and the analysis of compositional structure. 1904 was a pivotal year for Behrens and the school, when Dutch architect J.L. Mathieu Lauweriks joined the faculty. Lauweriks had evolved a systematic approach to teaching composition based on the dissection of a circle by a square, creating a grid of proportional spaces. Behrens saw that this system could be used to unify proportions within architecture and graphic design; in 1906, he applied this theory to his exhibition pavilion and poster for the Anchor Linoleum Company.

Rationalism, the Machine Aesthetic, and the Search for Universal Culture

In 1907, Behrens received a landmark design commission from the German electrical works, AEG, to be the company's artistic advisor. At the same time, he participated in the launching of the Deutsche Werkbund, or German Association of Craftsmen. Inspired by Morris but embracing, rather than rebelling against, the machine, the Werkbund sought to invent a universal culture through the design

of everyday objects and furnishings. Behrens's industrial-design projects through the Werkbund coincided with his association with AEG. In addition to designing AEG's teakettles and lighting fixtures, he also designed their visual identity, the first known design system for an industrial corporation. Beginning with its logo, he designed a company typeface, color schemes, posters, advertisements, salesrooms, and manufacturing facilities. Every item was articulated over a specific set of proportions and linear elements, organizing AEG's visual presentation into a harmonic whole.

Constructivism

The new visual language and its philosophy were attracting students and designers from abroad, as well as finding sympathetic participants. Russia's political upheaval of the early 1900s found a voice in abstraction; the pure geometry of a movement called Suprematism merged with Cubism and Futurism to generate Constructivism, an expression of Russia's quest for a new order. Seeking out instruction in Germany, a young Russian Constructivist, El (Lazar Markovich) Lissitsky, found himself in Darmstadt studying architecture, absorbing the rationalist aesthetic that was prevalent there. His studies kept him in Western Europe throughout World War I and for the duration of the Russian Revolution. In 1919, while the Bolsheviks were fighting for domination in the post-Tsarist civil war, Lissitsky went home and applied himself to politically driven graphic design that was characterized by dynamic, geometrically organized composition. His seminal poster, *Beat the Whites with the Red Wedge,* epitomizes the abstract communicative power of form and typifies the work of the Russian avant-garde from this period.

The Bauhaus and the New Order

As the war in Europe ended, designers and architects turned their attention to rebuilding and moving forward. In Germany, the 1919 reopening of the formerly prestigious Weimar Arts and Crafts School began with the appointment of architect Walter Gropius, one of Peter Behrens's former apprentices, as its new director. Gropius recast the school as the *Staatliches Bauhaus*—the State Home for Building. Here, experimentation and rationalism became the tools for building the new social order. Although the curriculum initially drew on expressionism—influenced by the *Blaue Reiter* painters who developed the preliminary training courses, Johannes Itten and Wassily Kandinsky—it gradually moved away from the personal and painterly.

The Bauhaus students and faculty became influenced by the Swiss painter Theo van Doesburg, whose de Stijl movement followed a strict dogma of geometry. Van Doesburg made contact with Gropius in 1920, and although Gropius decided against hiring him because of his overt dogma, van Doesburg contributed significantly to the aesthetic change in the Bauhaus by moving to Weimar and hosting discussions and lectures. Laszlo Moholy-Nagy, a Hungarian Constructivist, eventually replaced Itten as head of the preliminary course in 1923, when the Bauhaus moved to its new building in Dessau. In the type shop, Moholy's experimentation with asymmetrical layouts, photomontage, and elements from the type case expanded the geometric expression of Modernism in graphic

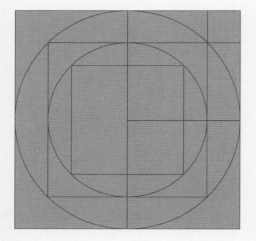

design. Moholy and a student, Herbert Bayer, used bars, rules, squares, and type asymmetrically composed on a grid as the basis of a new typography. Lissitsky returned from Russia numerous times, establishing contact with the Bauhaus and participating in lectures, book designs, and exhibitions. His 1924 book, *The Isms of Art,* is a watershed in grid development. Separated by heavy rules, the concurrently running text in three languages is organized into columns; images, captions, and folios are integrated into the overall structure, placed according to a distinct set of horizontal and vertical alignments.

Disseminating Asymmetry   As pervasive as these developments in design seem, they had yet to be assimilated into mainstream design practice. The use of asymmetric composition, sans serif typefaces, and geometric organization of information were known to a relative few in the arts and education. For the most part, the commercial world was oblivious. Developments in American and European advertising had helped introduced columnar composition into production of newspapers and periodicals; most printers and designers, however, were still visually in the nineteenth century. A young calligrapher, Jan Tschichold, changed that. While working as a staff designer for the German publisher Insel Verlag, Tschichold happened upon the first Bauhaus exhibition of 1923. Within a year he had assimilated the school's typographic approach and abstract sensibility. In 1925, he designed a twenty-four-page insert for the *Typographische Mitteilungen,* a German printers' magazine, which demonstrated these ideas to a large audience of typesetters, designers, and printers. "Elementare Typographie," as it was titled, generated a tremendous enthusiasm for asymmetric and grid-based layout.

Tschichold advocated a reductive and intrinsically functional aesthetic. He asserted that stripping away ornament, giving priority to sans serif type that made the structure of letterforms explicit, and creating compositions based on the verbal function of words were goals that would liberate the modern age. Negative spaces, the intervals between areas of text, and the orientation of words to each other formed the basis for design consideration. Taking his cues from Lissitsky and the Bauhaus, he deliberately built his compositions on a system of vertical and horizontal alignments, introducing hierarchical grid structure to order and creating space in documents from posters to letterheads. As early as 1927, the year before he published his landmark *Die Neue Typographie (The New Typography),* Tschichold codified this idea of structure and advocated its use to standardize printing formats. The current European DIN (*Deutsches Institut für Normung,* the German Institute for Standardization) system of paper formats—in which each format, folded in half, yields the next-smaller format—is based on this system.

Toward Neutrality   The developing design aesthetic in Europe was abruptly sidetracked, however, in the 1930s. Designers and artists who used the new visual language were arrested or forced to leave as the Nazis gained power and labeled them degenerates. The Bauhaus officially closed in 1932, and Moholy-Nagy, Gropius, Mies van der Rohe (Peter Behrens's other apprentice from before WWI), Bayer, and others left the continent for America; Tschichold, after being arrested and held by the Nazis for a short period, moved to Switzerland.

Switzerland remained neutral and generally unaffected by the war; its mountainous terrain and iron grip on international banking kept it safe from being overrun by the Nazis. The Swiss economy had gradually come to depend on services and craftsmanship that it could export; the country's small size had also deeply ingrained a famous determination to create order. Zurich and Basel were the cultural centers of the country; Zurich's banking and technology industries were the counterpart to Basel's thousand-year artistic heritage of drawing and book arts.

Neue Grafik and the Will to Order This more austere approach was also taken up by Josef Müller-Brockmann, Carlo Vivarelli, Hans Neuberg, and Richard Paul Lohse who, in their individual practices, were actively seeking a universal visual expression. As editors of the Zurich-published *Neue Grafik,* they collaborated in exposing this international style to the rest of the world. The grid created for *Neue Grafik* contained four columns and three horizontal bands, or spatial zones, which organized all of the content, including images. When it was first iterated, *Neue Grafik* marked a development in grid-based design that was already in the making: the realization of a module—a small unit of space which, through repetition, integrates all parts of a page. The width of a module defines a column-width, and its height defines the depth of paragraphs and, therefore, rows. Groups of modules are combined into zones that may be assigned a given purpose. In complex publishing projects, exhibits, and single-format posters, Müller-Brockmann and his colleagues developed modular systems from the content of their projects and implemented them with rigorous discipline. Müller-Brockmann forsook imagery in favor of pure constructions of type based on grids. In 1960, he published his first book *The Graphic Artist and His Design Problems* in which he first describes this form of grid-based design. His second book *Grid Systems in Graphic Design* is nothing short of a manifesto: "The grid system implies the will to systematize, to clarify, the will to penetrate to the essentials ... the will to cultivate objectivity rather than subjectivity."

Along with Tschichold, several Bauhaus students had come to Switzerland. Max Bill, who had begun school at the Kunstgewerbeschule in Zurich and had studied at the Bauhaus between 1927 and 1929, returned home in 1930; another Bauhaus student, Theo Ballmer, had also worked in the type shop. The influence of Ballmer, Tschichold, and Bill was strong. While Swiss designers had been developing a tradition that emphasized reductive techniques and simplification, that direction had focused on symbolic representation, epitomized by the work of *plakatstijl* designer Ernst Keller. Tschichold eventually turned to a classical typographic approach with more humanist attributes, but until the early 1940s he was still an advocate of asymmetry and grid-based composition. Ballmer and Bill continued to develop constructive ideas in their work based on strict mathematical measurement and spatial division. Max Bill's contribution was twofold: first, by applying his math-based theories to professional projects in advertising and corporate identity; and second, by instituting the grid through helping to found the Ulm School of Applied Arts in Germany in 1950. Bill's work and teaching would help to ingrain the grid in generations of designers.

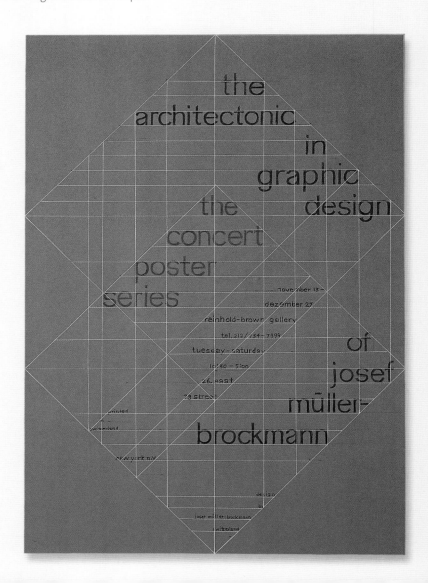

Grid Systems in
Graphic Design
Book spread
Josef Müller-Brockmann

Originally published by
Niggli Verlag, Zurich, 1962

The New Swiss Film
Poster
Josef Müller-Brockmann

Reproduced from *Grid Systems
in Graphic Design*, published
by Niggli Verlag, Zurich, 1962

Radikale Liste 1
Poster
Emil Ruder

Reproduced from *Typography*,
published by Niggli Verlag,
Zurich, 1960

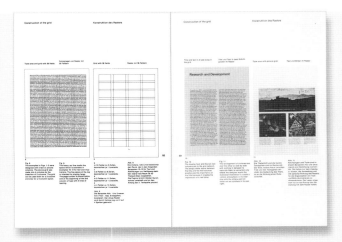

**für
einen geeinten
starken
sozialen
Kanton
Basel
Radikale
Liste
1**

Garanten
für eine gute
Verfassung:

The Basel School   In Basel, the *Allgemeine Gewerbeschule* (or Basel School of Design) was contributing to the development of the International Style through an approach that appeared to be somewhat at odds with that of Zurich designers. Its director, Armin Hoffmann, had been a student of Ernst Keller's, and fostered an intuitive method of composition based on symbolic form and contrasts between optical qualities in abstraction: light and dark, curve and angle, organic and geometric. Integrating type with image played an important role in the school's curriculum, however. In 1947, Zurich-trained Emil Ruder joined the AGS as a typography teacher. Ruder advocated a balance between form and function, rigorously exploring the nuances of typeface and optical contrast in addition to systematic, overall grid structures. His methodology instilled an exhaustive process of visual problem solving in his students that helped further the dissemination of the grid. One of these many students was Karl Gerstner, who went on to form his own practice in Zurich and contributed to the evolution of the grid into a mainstay of modern design practice. In 1968, Gerstner published his first book, *Designing Programmes.* "The typographic grid," he wrote, "is a proportional guideline for text, tables, pictures, etc. It is a formal program a priori for 'x' unknown contents. The problem: to find the balance between a maximum of conformity with a maximum of freedom. Or: the highest number of constants combined with the greatest possible variability."

The Corporate Grid   Grid use began to dominate European and American design during and after the 1960s. It was an especially effective way to orchestrate communications programs for large organizations, events, or corporations. Max Bill, Müller-Brockmann, Otl Aicher, and other exponents of the International Style were joined in their efforts by their Dutch, English, Italian, German, and American counterparts. In the Netherlands, the movement toward rational, program-oriented design was spearheaded by Wim Crouwel, Ben Bos, and Bruno Wissing, whose firm Total Design became a model in its practice of grid-based communications programs for corporations and cultural institutions. In America, students of the Swiss schools and a number of European emigrants were bringing

the International Style—and the grid—to a vast audience. Paul Rand, the pioneer of Modern design in America in the early 1940s, had been instrumental in convincing business that design was good for them; his clients and those of other designers had gradually become familiar with the idea of systems to help organize their public images. In his 1965 design manuals for Westinghouse, Rand developed complex grids to ensure continuity in such diverse media as packaging, print advertising, and television. The German designer Otl Aicher implemented a program of even greater precision for Lufthansa, the German airline. Collaborating with Tomás Gonda, Fritz Quereng, and Nick Roericht, Aicher anticipated Lufthansa's every potential need, standardizing formats and rigorously enforcing the grid to unify communications of different scale, materials, and production constraints. Detailed manuals and measurements ensured visual uniformity in every application.

The idea of a totality in design, based on a grid, also found expression in the work of Massimo Vignelli and his wife, Lella, who had founded an office for design in Milan in 1960. Both trained as architects, they established their vision of a seamlessly organized, systematic structural approach early in their careers. Massimo, in particular, had begun extensive exploration of grid structures for various cultural organizations and corporate entities in Milan. These early projects guided Vignelli toward an approach that focused on dividing space within a modular grid into semantically distinct zones. The additional system of division allowed greater focus within the overall modular structure, helping to clarify complex informational material. By giving these horizontal divisions visual weight in the form of solid bands, the eye could be taught to direct itself to find specific information. Vignelli helped found the design collaborative Unimark International in 1965, following his belief that design should reject the individual impulse for expression in favor of developing overall systems. Growing to roughly four hundred employees in forty-eight countries, Unimark systematized and standardized communications for a legion of corporate giants, among them Xerox, J.C. Penney, Alcoa, Ford, and Steelcase. In 1971, Massimo and Lella established Vignelli Associates in New York after Unimark disbanded. Their new company pursued a similar philosophy; the grid formed

Design in Michigan
Poster, one of a series
Katherine McCoy
Courtesy of Katherine McCoy

Citibank
Corporate identity manual
Anspach Grossman Portugal
Courtesy Enterprise IG

Octavo
Publication
8vo
Courtesy of Simon Johnston

By the late 1970s, formatting corporate communications in a grid was an expected approach to achieving visual continuity. Corporate identity firms like Anspach Grossman Portugal in New York City typified this approach with its 1976 identity program for Citibank and similar corporate clients. The International Style had come to be an accepted part of what graphic design was about. Designers also began to use the grid as an end in itself, and they exploited the visual potential of the form for its own sake. Radical experimentation based on grid structures during the 1980s and 1990s eventually led to examination of other kinds of organizational methods; designers and design educators like April Greiman (who studied typography in Basel) and Katherine McCoy (an industrial designer who came to graphic design through an early stint at Unimark), spearheaded explorations outside the realm of rational structure. This kind of deconstruction was also eventually assimilated into common practice alongside strictly grid-based work and other entirely antistructural ideas.

The grid has come to be seen as one of many tools that designers can use to help them communicate. In the 1980s and 1990s, the British design group 8vo helped reestablish awareness of structural thinking through their periodical journal *Octavo*, which addressed typographical issues in a series of eight editions. Amidst a proliferation of new approaches that owes some debt to the digital revolution, newer firms like MetaDesign, Una, and Method have steadfastly continued to investigate organizational methods that derive from the International Style.

As we move into the twenty-first century, the use of grids that developed in Europe over the last 150 years has continued to play a role in graphic design. The Internet has proven to be a medium that can benefit from grid-based thinking as a way of simplifying the vertiginous act of navigating through interactive information. How media and design will develop over the next 150 years is difficult to imagine, given its recent pace—but the typographic grid is likely to help designers structure communications for some time to come.

the underpinning of many of their endeavors in corporate identity, publication, and book design and interiors. In 1977, as part of the United States Government's Federal Design Improvement Program, Vignelli developed a system to unify publications for the National Park Service. Called Unigrid, the system established a modular grid, divided by horizontal bands, which encompassed twelve formats and could be imposed on a single standard-sized sheet of paper. This organization reduced paper waste, production time, and a number of other problems, allowing individual designers within and outside the National Park Service to concentrate on the creative aspects of designing individual brochures and posters.

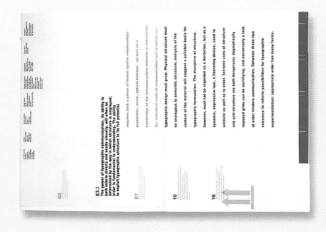

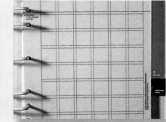

Henry Magaziner
Typography exercises
Students of Chris Myers,
University of the Arts,
Philadelphia:

Adam Hetherington
Nikki Scoggins
Jesse Taing

Grid Basics
A Workshop in Structural Designing

All design work involves problem solving on both visual and organizational levels. Pictures and symbols, fields of text, headlines, tabular data: all these pieces must come together to communicate. A grid is simply one approach to bringing those pieces together. Grids can be loose and organic, or they can be rigorous and mechanical. To some designers, the grid represents an inherent part of the craft of designing, the same way joinery in furniture making is a part of that particular craft. The history of the grid has been part of an evolution in how graphic designers think about designing, as well as a response to specific communication and production problems that needed to be solved. A corporate literature program, for example, is a late twentieth-century problem with complex goals and requirements. Among other things, a grid is suited to helping solve communication problems of great complexity.

The benefits of working with a grid are simple: clarity, efficiency, economy, and continuity.

Before anything else, a grid introduces systematic order to a layout, distinguishing types of information and easing a user's navigation through them. Using a grid permits a designer to lay out enormous amounts of information, such as in a book or a series of catalogues, in substantially less time because many design considerations have been addressed in building the grid's structure. The grid also allows many individuals to collaborate on the same project, or on series of related projects over time, without compromising established visual qualities from one project to the next.

How do grids work?
When are they appropriate?
Why use them at all?

Exploring the basics of typographic construction helps yield an understanding of the dynamic visual qualities that are inherent in the forms themselves. Within the format, alignments between elements create structure. In these compositions, space is divided based on content: like information is grouped together, disparate information is separated. Changes in weight and scale introduce hierarchy—visual ordering—to the information. Sometimes the kind of information listed in a particular column is called out through the use of bolder weight; sometimes a shift in alignment signals a change in importance. Within strict limitations, an enormous variety of possible layouts can be imagined. These, for example, all use the same type family and many of them use one size.

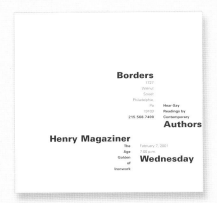

Breaking the Page into Parts   Building an effective grid for a given project means thoughtfully assessing that project's specific content in terms of the visual and semantic qualities of typographic space.

Typographic space is governed by a series of part-to-whole relationships. The single letter is a kernel, part of a word. Words together create a line: not just a line of thought but a line on the page, a visual element that establishes itself in the spatial field of the format. Placing a line of type in the blank landscape of a page instantly creates a structure. It's a simple structure, but one with a direction, a movement and, now, two defined areas of space: one space above the line and one space below.

One line after another, after another, becomes a paragraph. It's no longer simply a line, but a shape with a hard and a soft edge. The hard edge creates a reference to the page, and as it stretches out in depth, the paragraph becomes a column, simultaneously breaking space and becoming a space in itself. Columns repeated or varied in proportion create a rhythm of interlocking spaces in which the format edge is restated, countered, and restated again. The voids between paragraphs, columns, and images help to establish the eye's movement through the material, as do the textural mass of the words they surround.

Alignments between masses and voids visually connect or separate them. By breaking space within the compositional field, the designer stimulates and involves the viewer. A passive composition, where intervals between elements are regular, creates a field of texture that is in stasis. By introducing changes, such as a larger interval between lines or a heavier weight, the designer creates emphasis within the textural uniformity. The mind perceives that emphasis as some kind of importance. Creating importance establishes an order, or hierarchy, between elements on the page, and each successive change introduces a new relationship between the parts. Visual shifts in emphasis within the hierarchy are inseparable from their effect on the verbal or conceptual sense of the content. A designer has unlimited options for making changes in type size, weight, placement, and interval to affect hierarchy and, therefore, the perceived sequence of the information. The grid organizes this relationship of alignments and hierarchies into an intelligible order that is repeatable and understandable by others.

Anatomy of a Grid: The Basic Parts of a Page

A grid consists of a distinct set of alignment-based relationships that act as guides for distributing elements across a format. Every grid contains the same basic parts, no matter how complex the grid becomes. Each part fulfills a specific function; the parts can be combined as needed, or omitted from the overall structure at the designer's discretion, depending on how they interpret the informational requirements of the material.

Building an Appropriate Structure Working with a grid depends on two phases of development. In the first phase, the designer attempts to assess the informational characteristics and the production requirements of the content. This phase is extremely important; the grid is a closed system once it is developed, and in building it the designer must account for the content's idiosyncrasies, such as multiple kinds of information, the nature of the images, and the number of images. Additionally, the designer must anticipate potential problems that might occur while laying out the content within the grid, such as unusually long headlines, cropping of images, or dead spots left if the content in one section runs out.

The second phase consists of laying out the material according to the guidelines established by the grid. It's important to understand that the grid, although a precise guide, should never subordinate the elements within it. Its job is to provide overall unity without snuffing out the vitality of the composition. In most circumstances, the variety of solutions for laying out a page within a given grid are inexhaustible, but even then it's wise to violate the grid on occasion. A designer shouldn't be afraid of his or her grid, but push against it to test its limits. A really well-planned grid creates endless opportunities for exploration.

Every design problem is different and requires a grid structure that addresses its particular elements. There are several basic kinds of grid, and as a starting point, each is suited to solving certain kinds of problems. The first step in the process is to consider which type of basic structure will accommodate the project's specific needs.

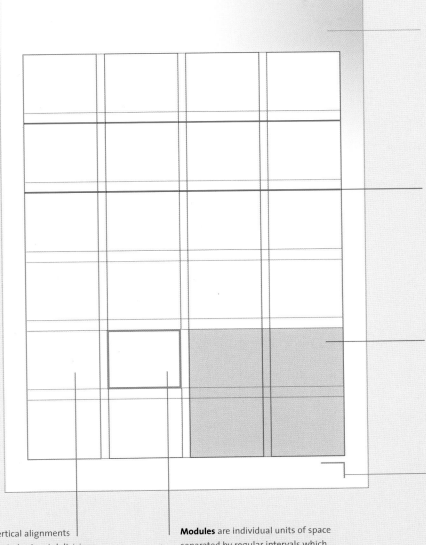

Margins are the negative spaces between the format edge and the content, which surround and define the live area where type and images will be arranged. The proportions of the margins bear a great deal of consideration, as they help establish the overall tension within the composition. Margins can be used to focus attention, serve as a resting place for the eye, or act as an area for subordinate information.

Flowlines are alignments that break the space into horizontal bands. Flowlines help guide the eye across the format and can be used to impose additional stopping and starting points for text or images.

Spatial zones are groups of modules that together form distinct fields. Each field can be assigned a specific role for displaying information; for example, a long horizontal field might be reserved for images, and the field below it might be reserved for a series of text columns.

Markers are placement indicators for subordinate or consistently appearing text, like running heads, section titles, folios, or any other element that occupies only one location in any layout.

Columns are vertical alignments of type that create horizontal divisions between the margins. There can be any number of columns; sometimes they are all the same width, and sometimes they are different widths corresponding to specific information.

Modules are individual units of space separated by regular intervals which, when repeated across the page format, create columns and rows.

Simple variations in margin size hint at the possibilities in this simplest of grid types.

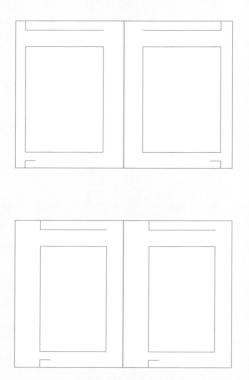

Dramatic margins create unexpected interest within this otherwise conventional manuscript grid.

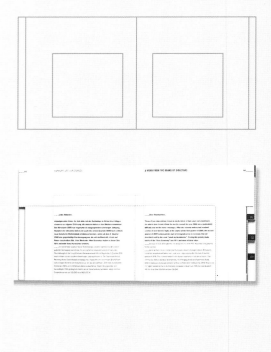

Manuscript Grid

The block, or manuscript, grid is structurally the simplest kind of grid. As its name implies, its base structure is a large rectangular area that takes up most of the page. Its job is to accommodate extensive continuous text, like a book or long essay, and it developed from the tradition of written manuscript that eventually led to book printing. It has a primary structure—the text block and the margins that define its position on a page—as well as a secondary structure that defines other essential details—the locations and size relationships of the running header or footer, chapter title, and page numbers, along with an area for footnotes, if appropriate.

Even within such a simple structure, care must be taken so the continuous type-texture can be read comfortably page after page. A large volume of type is essentially a passive gray composition. Creating visual interest, comfort, and stimulation is important to continuously engage the reader and to keep the eye from tiring too rapidly during long reading sessions.

Adjusting the proportions of the margins is one way of introducing visual interest. Within a two-page spread, the interior margins have to be wide enough to prevent the text from disappearing down into the gutter. Classical grids mirror the text blocks left and right around a wider gutter margin. Some designers use a mathematical ratio to determine a harmonic balance between the margins and the weight of the text block. In general, wider margins help focus the eye and create a sense of calm or stability. Narrow lateral margins increase tension because the live matter is in closer proximity to the format edge. Although traditional manuscript grids use margins that are symmetrical in width, it's just as acceptable to create an asymmetrical structure, wherein the margin intervals are different. An asymmetrical structure introduces more white space for the eye to use as an area of rest; it may also provide a place for notes, spot illustrations, or other editorial features that don't occur regularly and, therefore, don't really warrant the articulation of a true column.

The size of the text type in the block—as well as the space between lines, words, and treatments of subordinate material—is of incredible importance. Considering the size of the text type and its spacing characteristics allows the designer to add additional visual interest by treating the subordinate material in contrasting yet subtle ways. Remember that tiny shifts in typographic color, emphasis, or alignment create enormous differences in how they're perceived in the overall hierarchy of the page; in this case, less is usually more effective.

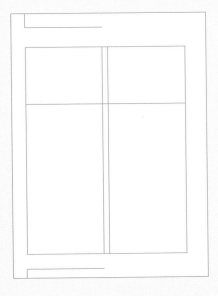

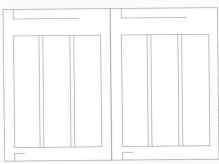

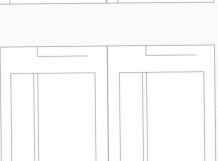

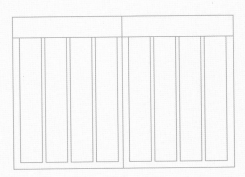

Three-column grids and asymmetrical one/two-column grids are common in editorial layout.

A precise four-column grid doesn't necessarily preclude dynamic layout. In this particular spread, the scale change of typographic elements is a foil to the grid.

Column Grid

Information that is discontinuous benefits from being organized into an arrangement of vertical columns. Because the columns can be dependent on each other for running text, independent for small blocks of text, or crossed over to make wider columns, the column grid is very flexible and can be used to separate different kinds of information. For example, some columns may be reserved for running text and large images, while captions may be placed in an adjacent column: this arrangement clearly separates the captions from the primary material, but allows the designer to create a direct relationship between the captions and the primary material.

The width of the columns depends on the size of the running text type. The goal is to find a width that accommodates a comfortable number of characters in one line of type at a given size. If the column is too narrow, excessive hyphenation is likely, and it will be difficult to achieve a uniform rag. At the other extreme, a column that is too wide for a given point size will make it difficult for the reader to find the beginnings of sequential lines. By studying the effects of changing the type size, leading, and spacing, the designer will be able to find a comfortable column width. In a traditional column grid, the gutter between columns is given a measure, x, and the margins are usually assigned a width of twice the gutter measure, or $2x$. Margins that are wider than the column gutters focus the eye inward, easing tension between the column edge and the edge of the format. There are no rules, however, and designers are free to adjust the column-to-margin ratio to suit their tastes or intentions.

In a column grid, there is also a subordinate structure. These are the flowlines: vertical intervals that allow the designer to accommodate unusual breaks in text or image on the page and create horizontal bands across the format. The hangline is one kind of flowline: the topmost capline of the running text content. It defines the vertical distance from the top of the format at which column text will always start. Sometimes, a flowline near the top of the page establishes a position for running headers, the pagination, or section dividers; additional flowlines in the middle or toward the bottom of the format can establish areas that the designer decides are for images only or for different kinds of concurrent running text, like a timeline, a subarticle, or a pull-quote.

When several kinds of information being handled in juxtaposition are radically different from each other, one option is to design a distinct column grid for each kind instead of attempting to build a single column grid. The nature of the information to be displayed might require one component grid of two columns and a second grid of three columns, both with the same margins. In this compound column grid, the middle column of the three-column grid straddles the gutter between the columns of the two-column grid. A compound column grid can be made up of two, three, four, or more distinct component grids, each devoted to content of a specific type.

The Guardian
Newspaper
Pentagram UK

Headlines, pictures, and
captions are all streamlined
for production by this
newspaper's modular grid.

The Motown Album
Book
Sheila deBretteville

An enormous variety of
picture formats, text and
captions are unified in a
"scrapbook" presentation
in this picture book.

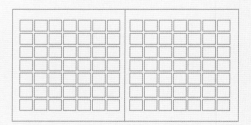

Modular Grid

Extremely complex projects require a degree of control beyond what a column grid will provide, and in this situation, a modular grid may be the most useful choice. A modular grid is essentially a column grid with a large number of horizontal flowlines that subdivide the columns into rows, creating a matrix of cells called *modules*. Each module defines a small chunk of informational space. Grouped together, these modules define areas called *spatial zones* to which specific roles may be assigned. The degree of control within the grid depends on the size of the modules. Smaller modules provide more flexibility and greater precision, but too many subdivisions can become confusing or redundant.

The module's proportions can be determined in any number of ways. Sometimes, for example, the module might be the width and depth of one average paragraph of the primary text at a given size. Modules can be vertical or horizontal in proportion, and this decision can be related to the kinds of images being organized or to the

desired overall stress the designer feels is most appropriate. The margin proportions must be considered simultaneously in relation to the modules and the gutters that separate them. Modular grids are most often used to coordinate extensive publication systems. If the designer has the opportunity to consider all (or most) of the materials that are intended to be produced within a system, the formats can become an outgrowth of the module or vice versa. By regulating the proportions of the formats and the module in relation to each other, the designer achieves several goals. The interrelationship of the formats means they can be used harmoniously together; the formats are more likely to be able to be produced simultaneously and, therefore, much more inexpensively.

A modular grid also lends itself to the design of tabular information, like charts, forms, schedules, or navigation systems. The rigorous repetition of the module helps to standardize space in tables or forms and can also help to integrate them with the structure of surrounding text and image material.

Aside from its practical uses, the modular grid has developed a conceptual, aesthetic image that some designers find attractive. Between the 1950s and 1980s, the modular grid became associated with ideal social or political order. These ideals have their roots in the rationalist thinking of the Bauhaus and Swiss International Style, which celebrate objectivity and order, reduction to essentials, and clarity of form and communication. Designers who embrace these ideals sometimes use modular grids to convey this rationalism as an interpretive overlay to a given communication. Even projects with simple informational needs or single formats can be structured with a rigid modular grid, adding additional meaning of order, clarity, and thoughtfulness or an urban, mathematical, or technological feel.

www.princetonart.org
Internet site
Swim Design

Web pages are the most
common example of hierarchic
grids. The alignments change
depending on the content but
remain proportionally integrated.

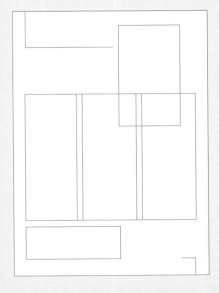

Hierarchical Grid

Sometimes the visual and informational needs
of a project require an odd grid that doesn't
fit into any category. These grids conform to the
needs of the information they organize, but
they are based more on an intuitive placement
of alignments customized to the various proportions of the elements, rather than on regular
repeated intervals. Column widths, as well as
the intervals between them, tend to vary.

Developing a hierarchical grid begins by studying
the various elements' optical interaction in
different positions spontaneously, and then by
determining a rationalized structure that will
coordinate them. Careful attention to the nuances
of weight change, size change, and position on
the page can yield an armature that is repeatable
over multiple pages. Sometimes a hierarchical
grid unifies disparate elements or creates a
superstructure that opposes organic elements
in a single-instance format like a poster. A hierarchical grid can also be used to unify sides of
packages or to create new visual arrangements
if they're displayed in groups.

Web pages are examples of hierarchical grids.
During the Web's early development, many of
the variables of Web-page composition were
unfixable because of the end user's browser
settings. Even today, with the control to establish
fixed margins, the dynamic content that drives
most Web sites, along with the continued
option of resizing the browser window, requires
a flexibility of width and depth that precludes
a strict modular approach, but still requires
a standardization, or templating, of alignments
and display areas.

This kind of grid, whether used to build books,
posters, or Web pages, is an almost organic
approach to the way information and elements
are ordered that still holds all of the parts
together architecturally in typographic space.

Variation and Violation
Sequencing in Grid-Based Layouts

A grid is truly successful only if, after all of the literal problems have been solved, the designer rises above the uniformity implied by its structure and uses it to create a dynamic visual narrative of parts that will sustain interest page after page. The greatest danger in using a grid is to succumb to its regularity. It's important to remember that the grid is an invisible guide that exists on the "bottommost level" of the layout; the content happens on top of it, sometimes constrained and sometimes free to move. Grids don't make dull layouts—designers do.

Once a grid is in place, it's a good idea to sort all of the project's material spread by spread to see how much is appearing in each. A storyboard of thumbnails for each spread in the project (or each frame of an animation or each Web page) can be very helpful for getting a sense of what content is going where, what content or imagery still needs to be developed, and what each spread will look like in tandem with the others. Here, the designer can test layout variations on the grid and see the result in terms of pacing— the rhythm of the layouts. Can there be a visual logic to how elements interact with the grid from page to page? For example, do pictorial elements alternate in position from one spread

to another? Is there a rhythm to how the overall darkness and lightness of each spread relates to the others? Perhaps there's a slow build from simple to more complex arrangements or a staggered, dynamic alternation of density over the range of spreads.

By creating a rhythmic or sequential logic among the spreads in the way they relate to the grid, each spread can have a distinct visual presentation but still work as part of the whole. The parts have unity imparted by the grid working underneath them.

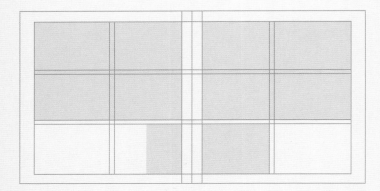

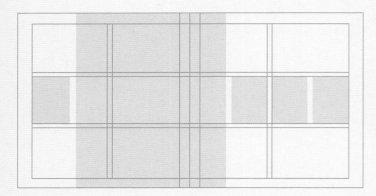

The effective use of a simple modular column grid is clearly demonstrated by the page spreads of this book. The grid is very regular, but the designer's use of alternating spatial zones for the locations of images from page to page accomplishes three goals: the variation in placement of images creates visual interest; it serves to reinforce the grid by making its presence known in multiple ways; and it creates a rhythmic sense of unity between the pages, a pacing and cadence that adds to the experience of reading and seeing.

Abstract
Architectural Journal
Willi Kunz Associates

The designer articulates this
modular grid in two distinct
ways to give character to individual sections. The page
spread at top shows building
models, diagrams, and notes
on a white field, where parcels
of information are rigorously
bound to the module's proportions. In the page spread below,
the module is subordinated
to dramatic divisions of space
where columnar information
and photographic images are
allowed to float in a dynamic,
indeterminate environment.

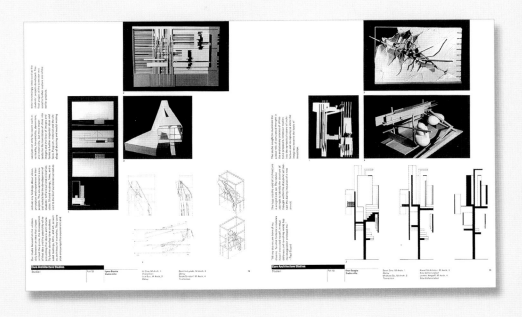

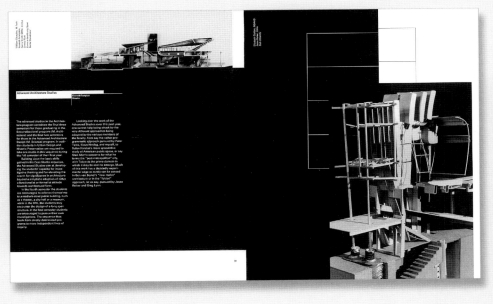

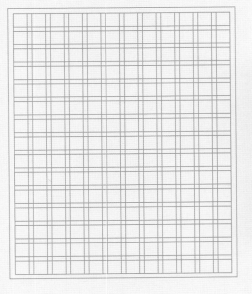

Key to Exhibit Notation

The diagram below shows a typical page spread for the Exhibit sections. The notations provided for each exhibit feature selected information for quick reference and a simple system for comparing related works in both sections (see also *Breaking the Grid, Exhibits*, page 128), grid-based or not.

These comparisons are meant as a catalyst for analysis. Sometimes the relationship between exhibits being compared is plainly structural, at other times it's less explicit; in some cases, the comparison is between exhibits that show opposing qualities.

Exhibit Number

Exhibit Credits

Section Marker

Exhibit Structure

Structural Diagram

Exhibit Comparisons
A listing of exhibits, color-coded by section, that are related

image area

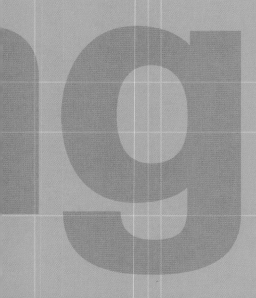

Exhibits
Grid-Based Design Projects

structure

Manuscript grid [overall], instances of column grid

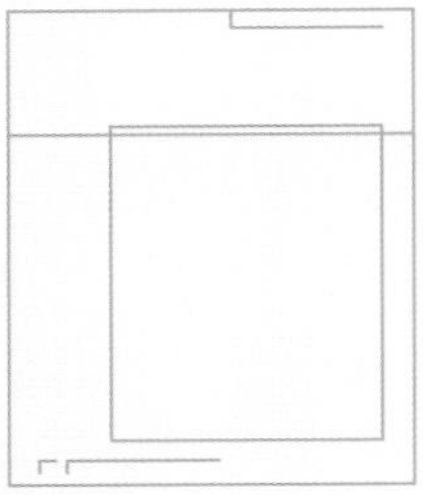

exhibit comparisons

12 15 21 34

01 14 27

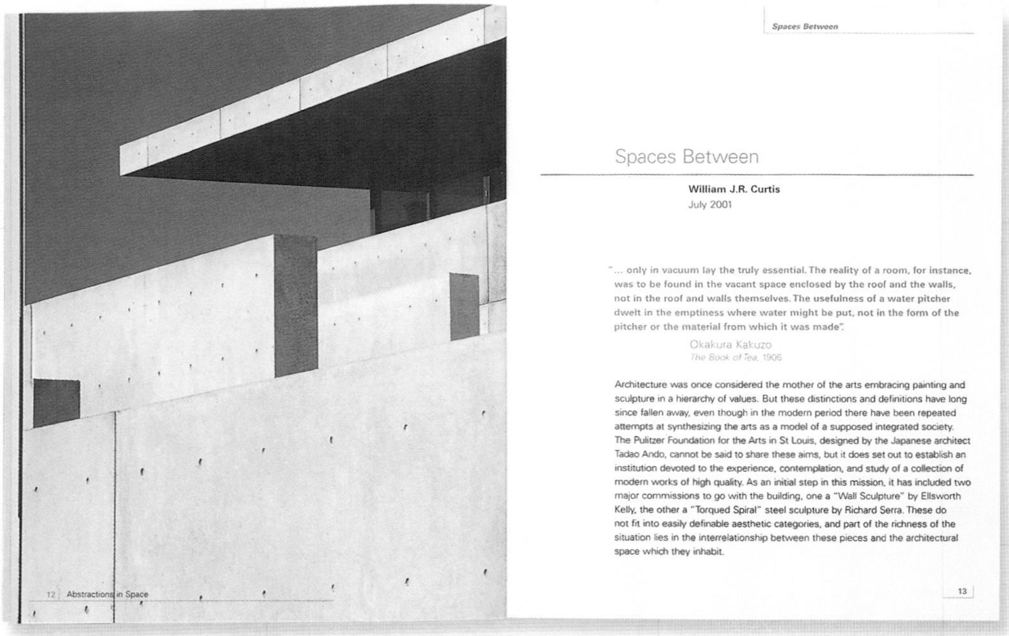

Spaces Between

William J.R. Curtis
July 2001

"... only in vacuum lay the truly essential. The reality of a room, for instance, was to be found in the vacant space enclosed by the roof and the walls, not in the roof and walls themselves. The usefulness of a water pitcher dwelt in the emptiness where water might be put, not in the form of the pitcher or the material from which it was made".

Okakura Kakuzo
The Book of Tea, 1906

Architecture was once considered the mother of the arts embracing painting and sculpture in a hierarchy of values. But these distinctions and definitions have long since fallen away, even though in the modern period there have been repeated attempts at synthesizing the arts as a model of a supposed integrated society. The Pulitzer Foundation for the Arts in St Louis, designed by the Japanese architect Tadao Ando, cannot be said to share these aims, but it does set out to establish an institution devoted to the experience, contemplation, and study of a collection of modern works of high quality. As an initial step in this mission, it has included two major commissions to go with the building, one a "Wall Sculpture" by Ellsworth Kelly, the other a "Torqued Spiral" steel sculpture by Richard Serra. These do not fit into easily definable aesthetic categories, and part of the richness of the situation lies in the interrelationship between these pieces and the architectural space which they inhabit.

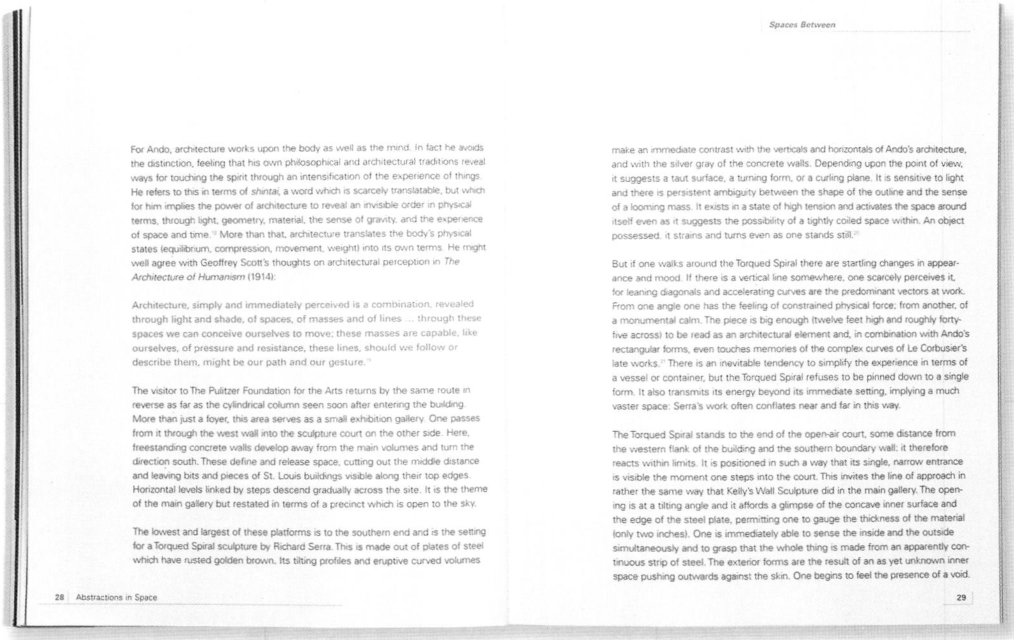

For Ando, architecture works upon the body as well as the mind. In fact he avoids the distinction, feeling that his own philosophical and architectural traditions reveal ways for touching the spirit through an intensification of the experience of things. He refers to this in terms of *shintai*, a word which is scarcely translatable, but which for him implies the power of architecture to reveal an invisible order in physical terms, through light, geometry, material, the sense of gravity, and the experience of space and time.[18] More than that, architecture translates the body's physical states (equilibrium, compression, movement, weight) into its own terms. He might well agree with Geoffrey Scott's thoughts on architectural perception in *The Architecture of Humanism* (1914):

Architecture, simply and immediately perceived is a combination, revealed through light and shade, of spaces, of masses and of lines ... through these spaces we can conceive ourselves to move; these masses are capable, like ourselves, of pressure and resistance, these lines, should we follow or describe them, might be our path and our gesture.[19]

The visitor to The Pulitzer Foundation for the Arts returns by the same route in reverse as far as the cylindrical column seen soon after entering the building. More than just a foyer, this area serves as a small exhibition gallery. One passes from it through the west wall into the sculpture court on the other side. Here, freestanding concrete walls develop away from the main volumes and turn the direction south. These define and release space, cutting out the middle distance and leaving bits and pieces of St. Louis buildings visible along their top edges. Horizontal levels linked by steps descend gradually across the site. It is the theme of the main gallery but restated in terms of a precinct which is open to the sky.

The lowest and largest of these platforms is to the southern end and is the setting for a Torqued Spiral sculpture by Richard Serra. This is made out of plates of steel which have rusted golden brown. Its tilting profiles and eruptive curved volumes make an immediate contrast with the verticals and horizontals of Ando's architecture, and with the silver gray of the concrete walls. Depending upon the point of view, it suggests a taut surface, a turning form, or a curling plane. It is sensitive to light and there is persistent ambiguity between the shape of the outline and the sense of a looming mass. It exists in a state of high tension and activates the space around itself even as it suggests the possibility of a tightly coiled space within. An object possessed, it strains and turns even as one stands still.[20]

But if one walks around the Torqued Spiral there are startling changes in appearance and mood. If there is a vertical line somewhere, one scarcely perceives it, for leaning diagonals and accelerating curves are the predominant vectors at work. From one angle one has the feeling of constrained physical force; from another, of a monumental calm. The piece is big enough (twelve feet high and roughly forty-five across) to be read as an architectural element and, in combination with Ando's rectangular forms, even touches memories of the complex curves of Le Corbusier's late works.[21] There is an inevitable tendency to simplify the experience in terms of a vessel or container, but the Torqued Spiral refuses to be pinned down to a single form. It also transmits its energy beyond its immediate setting, implying a much vaster space: Serra's work often conflates near and far in this way.

The Torqued Spiral stands to the end of the open-air court, some distance from the western flank of the building and the southern boundary wall: it therefore reacts within limits. It is positioned in such a way that its single, narrow entrance is visible the moment one steps into the court. This invites the line of approach in rather the same way that Kelly's Wall Sculpture did in the main gallery. The opening is at a tilting angle and it affords a glimpse of the concave inner surface and the edge of the steel plate, permitting one to gauge the thickness of the material (only two inches). One is immediately able to sense the inside and the outside simultaneously and to grasp that the whole thing is made from an apparently continuous strip of steel. The exterior forms are the result of an as yet unknown inner space pushing outwards against the skin. One begins to feel the presence of a void.

project
Abstractions in Space
Commemorative book
Perfect-bound
Paper cover with printed
vellum jacket
Text printed offset

client
Pulitzer Foundation
Arts organization and
museum
Saint Louis, MO

design
Lynn Fylak
New York, NY

photography
Robert Pettus
Saint Louis, MO

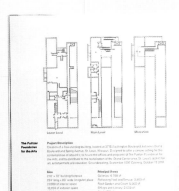

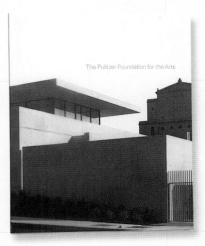

This small book celebrates the calming austerity of the architects and artists commissioned by the Pulitzer Foundation to create its new exhibition and museum space: Tadao Ando, the Japanese minimalist architect; Richard Serra, the American sculptor; and Ellsworth Kelly, the American painter. The book relies on a manuscript grid with a pronounced asymmetry. The left and top margins are dramatically wide, forcing the text block to the right and down. The effect of architectural solidity created by these proportions is offset by the serene, open quality of the margin. A constant hangline for running text, and a second—high above for the running head—create a quiet, simple structure that echoes the directness and purity of the real-world architecture the text describes.

Mirrored folios are bent toward asymmetry through the use of hairline rules that refer to the geometry in the building and paintings inside it. Images selected for their simplicity and abstract qualities are displayed in one of only two ways: bleeding off all sides of one page within a spread, or simply centered in a window whose proportion is defined by the leading corner of the grid's text block. The pacing is varied through stately alternation of the picture formats and black or white fields. Notes and floorplans are accommodated by a three-column grid dominated by the low hangline of the primary manuscript grid.

structure
Column grid

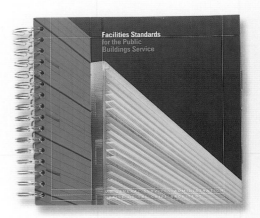

exhibit comparisons

02	05	08	11
12	14	18	22
26	28	33	36
37

04	05	07	09
10	13	15	16
22	23	30	31
33	36

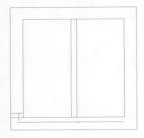

project
Standards manual
Structural and wayfinding
guidelines for public
architecture

Wire-bound book
Offset lithography

client
U.S. General Services
Administration
Government agency
Washington, DC

design
Chermayeff & Geismar
Associates
Keith Helmetag [AD]
New York, NY

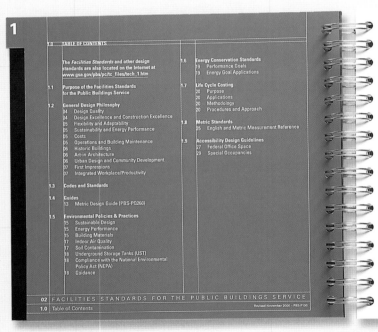

A very basic two-column grid organizes this guidelines manual. As a document that must serve a number of decentralized GSA (General Services Administration) and public-buildings development offices, its simplicity promotes continuity in approach and helps users access information easily. The columns roughly divide the pages in half. The margins are optically even; the interior margins are a bit wider to compensate for the ring binding. While linear elements demarcate the margins throughout, the full grid is made evident in the section contents pages as a reference to architectural blueprints.

Running section folios span the two columns, but at the foot of the page rather than at the top, giving precedence to the more important elements of the hierarchy: section headlines, subheads, and bulleted information.

Charts and tables are easily integrated into the grid and provide some variation within the straightforward page layouts. Tab dividers use the grid's margin frame as a decorative element, contrasting the large-scale section numerals and titles.

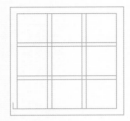

exhibit comparisons

diverse**city**

vivacity still celebrating the new

The show must go on and it did. Heralded with fireworks, parties and parades, the first year of the new Millennium continued with a non-stop extravaganza of the arts and of artists right across London. The Millennium Festival, funded by the National Lottery, broke all the rules by happening everywhere all the time – well into the summer of 2001. And last century's year-by-year focus on different artforms culminated in our new century with the *Year of the Artist*, which brought living artists together with a vast number of people in a wide variety of extraordinary places.

Since Carnival has become the most potent symbol of the colour, creativity and vitality of the arts in this most diverse of cities, the Carnival Gala at the Millennium Dome in August 2000 offers as good a start as any to this retrospective of a thrilling year. The Gala built on Carnival's central role in the Millennium Eve celebrations and attracted an audience of 4,000 to Greenwich, a huge increase on previous years. Many there felt this was the best yet: great bands, great costumes and a great show that captured the year's sense of celebration and renewed energy.

Equally emblematic of a city entering a new phase of confidence and enterprise was Tate Modern, the converted power station that provoked an unprecedented outpouring of enthusiasm for contemporary art. Far sooner than anyone expected, this world-class new gallery for London broke all records for public visitors.

The newly refurbished Royal Court created a different kind of buzz with its upstairs Studio Theatre showcasing a vast range of writers and plays from both home and abroad, including Sarah Kane's prescient *4:48 Psychosis, Mr Kolpert* by young German playwright David

Gieselmann and Caryl Churchill's *Far Away*, which subsequently transferred to the West End.

Smaller in scale but often with ambitions at least as big, a clutch of other new and refurbished buildings opened up for business across the city. Soho Theatre and Writers' Centre was just one. With its central location and its young audiences, the venue not only puts on new writing in the main theatre but helps to make it happen in the first place. With around 2,000 scripts to read a year, it has 60 writers enrolled on a development programme that opens up studio-space for workshops and readings and offers rooms equipped just for people to come and write.

The year also brought reminders that all these new developments have their roots in decades or more of faith, hope and charitable giving. One signal event was the centenary exhibition at the Whitechapel Art Gallery, an institution that has a record of reaching out to people and bringing them in to see what the arts have to offer.

Opening moves

Coinciding with all this celebratory activity was the election in May 2000 of Ken Livingstone, London's first ever mayor, and the creation of the Greater London Authority (GLA). The GLA

has a commitment to developing a cultural strategy for the new Millennium. Kidslink was an early project launched by the Mayor. This scheme to engage 7-11 year olds in London with cultural events and institutions was developed by London 2000 with London Arts as a partner and funder of the enterprise. Hosted and managed by the London Tourist Board, the project twinned over 170 primary schools with London attractions and venues. As well as going on free visits, pupils reviewed the attractions in words and pictures, posting them on a website with links to www.londontouristboard.com, now the capital's main visitor website. Like many other Millennium initiatives, Kidslink has left a positive legacy, inspiring a new scheme from the GLA offering school groups free travel to cultural events and venues.

The epicentre of the Millennium celebrations was Greenwich. The borough has undergone a cultural renaissance with the development of the new Laban Centre on its border, the relocation of Trinity College of Music, the renewal of the Woolwich Arsenal, the development of creative industries in the Thames Gateway area, and a major arts and regeneration project with Lewisham and the National Theatre. In recognition of

The design of this annual report uses a direct, large-scale grid, three modules high by three wide, within a square format. The effect is disarmingly simple, but it permits the designers to bring unity to the everchanging types of art, photography, and activities that will be showcased on behalf of the client, a philanthropic arts organization.

project
Annual Report
Perfect-bound book
Paper cover with die cut
Offset lithography

client
London Arts
Arts philanthropic
organization
London, England

design
Why Not Associates
London, England

photography
Adrian Fisk
London, England

> "The idea of a 'mobile' residency was intriguing for a couple of reasons. First, I repeatedly find myself telling cab drivers things I wouldn't ordinarily dream of telling a stranger. And they tell me their stories as well … That leads to the second, more important reason: London's mini-cabs are driven largely by immigrants. And I'm an immigrant a few times over."
>
> Ian Iqbal Rashid, writer, about his *Back Routes* residency for the *Year of the Artist*

capacity investing in the creative spirit

How creative can a cheque be? That question is the bottom line for any funder. In the arts – where the sky is barely the limit – it is crucial to make investments that really count, now and in the long-term. This means partnerships with other funders and policy-makers, strategic approaches to specific needs – and finding other ways to support the arts other than simply writing cheques. This year London Arts worked to achieve Lottery capital awards for many excellent projects. Detailed reviews resulted in greater support for some sectors, notably theatre, and the creation of entirely new projects, including a literature development agency for West London.

The three-column modules are spanned by type and image in alternating combinations of one, two, and three module widths for a lively visual rhythm of blocks and bands, sometimes one module row deep, sometimes two, or sometimes all three. The modules are separated by a generous gutter that enhances the modular quality and calls attention to the shapes created by the text and images. Pull quotes in larger type, running text, informational listings, and financial data all adhere to the grid. Dramatic cropping and compositional elements within the photographs shown alleviate regularity and visually interact with the modular architecture of the pages.

structure
Hierarchical grid

exhibit comparisons

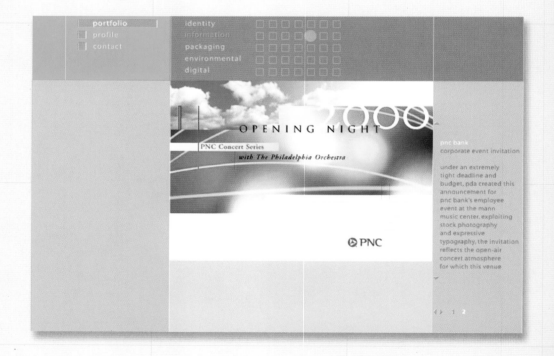

project
www.paonedesign.com
Internet site
Flash version 5.0

client
Paone Design Associates
Graphic designers
Philadelphia, PA

design
Paone Design Associates
Gregory Paone
Philadephia, PA

programming
Juan Sensenanea
Madrid, Spain

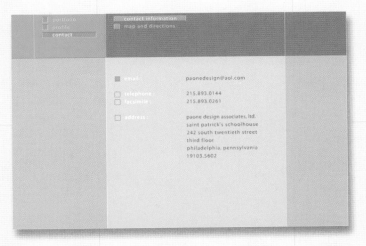

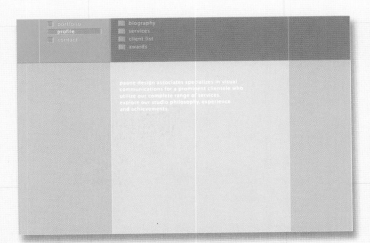

A simple hierarchical grid organizes the marketing and portfolio content for this design firm's own Internet site. The proportions of each area within the page correspond to the function of that area in managing content. The major horizontal divisions, for example, separate a large area for text and images. None of the content areas are the same proportion, but their respective horizontal, vertical, and modular dimensions hold each other in a quiet sort of tension.

The grid's division lines are left showing, and provide a subtle visual language to unite the branding and navigation treatments.

The square format of the main content frame can hold different formats of the design firm's work, from long brochures to individual logos. The hangline separates the navigation, branding, and detail-view areas from the primary content area where the firm's projects are shown.

exhibit comparisons

Stichting Preferente aandelen C Van Lanschot

Stichting Preferente aandelen C Van Lanschot, 's-Hertogenbosch, was founded on 28 December 1999. The Stichting and Van Lanschot have entered into a call option agreement under which the Stichting is entitled to take preference shares C up to a maximum of 50% of the share capital of Van Lanschot NV outstanding before exercising the call option. Furthermore, a put option agreement has been concluded between the Stichting and Van Lanschot NV under which Van Lanschot NV has the right to issue preference shares C in the capital of Van Lanschot NV to the Stichting up to a maximum of 50% of the nominal share capital issued in the form of ordinary shares, preference shares A and preference shares B, or, if the issue takes place with the prior approval of the Annual General Meeting of Shareholders of Van Lanschot NV, as many additional shares as agreed between the parties.

At least 25% of the nominal value of the preference shares C must be paid up on issue.

The members of the Board are:

A.A.M. Deterink *Chairman*
J.V.H. Pennings *Deputy Chairman*
F.H.J. Boons
C.W. de Monchy
H.J. Baeten

Statement of independence

The Board of Stichting Preferente aandelen C Van Lanschot and the Board of Managing Directors of Van Lanschot NV hereby declare that in their joint opinion the requirements of Appendix X of the Listing and Issuing Rules of Euronext Amsterdam NV, Amsterdam, have been satisfied in respect of the independence of the members of the Board of Stichting Preferente aandelen C Van Lanschot.

Stichting Preferente aandelen C Van Lanschot   Van Lanschot NV
The Board   The Board of Managing Directors
's-Hertogenbosch, 19 February 2001

Report of the Supervisory Board

We take pleasure in presenting the shareholders with the Annual Report 2000 of Van Lanschot NV, which includes the Report of the Board of Managing Directors and the annual accounts of Van Lanschot NV. The annual accounts have been audited by Ernst & Young Accountants and adopted by our Board without amendment.

We propose that the Annual General Meeting of Shareholders approve the 2000 annual accounts as submitted and endorse the Board of Managing Directors' conduct of the Bank's affairs and the Supervisory Board's supervision thereof, as evidenced by the annual accounts and the Report of the Board of Managing Directors. On approval of the annual accounts and the profit appropriation contained therein, € 41.9 million will be distributed by way of dividend and € 105.9 million will be taken to reserves. Holders of ordinary shares will receive an optional stock dividend of € 1.35 per share of € 1.00 nominal. Other shareholders will receive the dividend stated on page 79 of this Annual Report in accordance with the Articles of Association.

At the Annual General Meeting of 12 May 2000, Messrs H. Langman, H.J. Bierma, P.C. van Gool and T.J. Peeters, who had stood down from the Supervisory Board by rotation, were reappointed for a new term of office. At the end of the year, our Board received the sad news that Mr van Gool had died after a brief illness, robbing the Board of an expert and experienced member. We shall hold dear the memory of Mr van Gool's warm personality and his contribution to our Board's deliberations. A decision has not yet been taken on filling the resultant vacancy.

The Supervisory Board met on five occasions during the year under review. Standard items on the agenda included the annual and interim figures, the business plan and the budgets. The annual accounts, the auditors' report and the management letter were discussed in the presence of the external auditors. Further subjects considered were the progress of the large IT projects, the Private Banking strategy and the performance of Van Lanschot Belgium, such with the aid of presentations given by the relevant group managing directors. The Board also considered developments on the financial markets and risk management. In addition, the Board studied the annual rating report on the Bank and discussed the Bank's human resources policy and staff developments during the year. It also held the annual meeting with the Chairman of the Board of Managing Directors to discuss the Board of Managing Directors' performance. The performance of the Supervisory Board was discussed in the absence of the Board of Managing Directors.

Both the Audit and Compliance Committee and the Credit and Risk Committee, which are both made up of Supervisory Board members, met on three occasions during the year. By way of preparation for the full Supervisory Board meeting, the Audit and Compliance

---

Van Lanschot in 2000

For Van Lanschot, 2000 was another year of significant growth in its operating profit and the volume of its business. The Bank's total assets increased by more than € 1.5 billion, or 18.6%, to € 9.7 billion, while operating profit after taxation advanced by € 18.3 million, or 29.3%, to € 80.8 million. Furthermore, extraordinary income for the year was realised of € 67.1 million. Net profit consequently more than doubled in comparison with 1999, which itself had been a highly successful year. Earnings per ordinary share before extraordinary income rose by € 0.59 or 27.8% to € 2.71.

The operating profit was particularly satisfactory in view of the hard work dedicated to strengthening the Bank's position during the year. A great deal of effort was put into modernising and expanding our information systems; following the expansion of the Internet service in 2000 to provide information to clients, for example, a project to enable clients to place securities orders over the Internet is now at an advanced stage. Staff training, marketing and communication also had high priority, partly in anticipation of the introduction of the new tax regime in the Netherlands in 2001.

Significant progress was also made with regard to accommodation. In spring 2000 the 'Van Lanschot Tower' was taken into service in 's-Hertogenbosch to house the greatly expanded central securities activities and a number of support services. A start was also made during the year on the partial renovation of the head office on Hooge Steenweg, the branches in The Hague and Waalwijk were substantially enlarged and stylish new branches were opened in Breda and Nijmegen. Furthermore, construction, renovation and expansion projects were started in Courtrai, Almere, Tilburg and Rotterdam and new premises were purchased in Goes, Brussels, Hasselt (Belgium), Zeist, Dordrecht and Zwolle.

The extension of Van Lanschot's commercial reach, which was reflected chiefly in the 12% rise in the average number of staff, significantly increased the number of target group accounts in both the corporate and the private markets. In the Netherlands, the number of corporate accounts increased by 14% to more than 4,400 and the number of private target group accounts by 11% to more than 42,500. In Belgium, the number of accounts rose by 9% to nearly 2,400; practically all the new clients are high net-worth Belgians. Including all the foreign branches, the number of private target group accounts at 31 December 2000 was nearly 48,000, in comparison with 43,600 a year previously.

General economic conditions were excellent during the year, although circumstances on some of Van Lanschot's markets may not necessarily have been as good. The growth in securities commission income eased in the second half of the year as the stock exchanges weakened in the last six months. In the home mortgage loans market, margins tightened during the same period and competition intensified. Aided by the sound economic climate,

In thousands of euros			
Results	**2000**	**1999**	**Change**
Interest	148,550	135,128	9.9%
Participating interests with influence	567	1,380	(58.9%)
Participating interests without influence	482	484	(0.4%)
Dividend from other participating interests	6,413	6,402	0.3%
Equity shares in investment portfolio	2,348	1,418	65.6%
Income from securities and participating interests	9,819	9,684	1.4%
Insurance commission	15,748	12,507	25.9%
Commission on documentary transactions	2,114	1,863	13.5%
Securities commission	151,600	111,886	35.5%
Commission on cash transactions and payment transfers	10,822	10,361	4.5%
Other commission	8,074	6,972	15.8%
Commission	188,158	143,589	31.0%
Capital gains on securities	6,081	997	510.0%
Foreign exchange gains	8,223	4,139	98.6%
Share in profit of other participating interests	(1,438)	1,000	(152.0%)
Other profit /(loss) on financial transactions	245	(139)	277.0%
Profit on financial transactions	13,111	7,897	67.3%
Total income	359,738	296,298	21.5%
Staff costs	109,149	107,306	20.4%
Other administrative expenses	86,463	71,507	20.9%
Depreciation	13,713	11,885	16.0%
Operating expenses	209,325	189,698	20.9%
Value adjustments to receivables	8,157	7,835	4.1%
Addition to Fund for general banking risks	6,591	6,912	(4.6%)
Total expenses	144,073	204,363	12.4%
Operating profit before taxation	115,665		

project
Annual Report 2000
Casebound book
Embossed paperboard cover
Silkscreened jacket
Text printed offset, two colors

client
Van Lanschot Bank
Financial services
Amsterdam, Netherlands

design
UNA [Amsterdam]
Designers
Hans Bockting
Sabine Reinhardt
Amsterdam, Netherlands

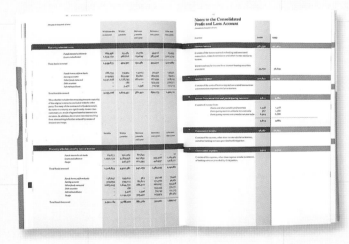

This annual report for a private bank in the Netherlands is organized around an elegant column grid that seamlessly integrates running text, tables, and financial disclosures.

The text block is divided into four primary columns of 40 mm each, and those again in half—the width of the longest numeric figure in any table. A set of alignments separated by 10 mm at the leading edge of the main text block provides a consistent edge for text and financials, and subheads or notations outdent slightly to align with the page number up top.

The hangline for body text creates a space between the running title head that orients the tabular matter. Columns of numbers are differentiated by white space or background tints, with the Year 2000 figures given the most prominence.

The hard cover is embossed with the bank's family crest in a nod to its reserved interior, but is wrapped by a colorful, folded poster that displays the most relevant financial figures from the interior. The lively composition is an attractive departure from the stately interior structure, but the short-folded edge that reveals the bank's logotype echoes the hangline from inside the report.

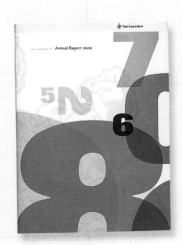

project
A Colorful New Year
Promotional poster
Seven-color silkscreen

client
Bösch Siebdruck AG
Commercial silkscreen
printers
Willisau, Switzerland

design
Niklaus Troxler Design
Niklaus Troxler
Willisau, Switzerland

structure
Modular grid

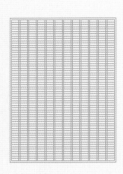

exhibit comparisons

03	07	10	13
16	17	19	22
24	25	27	29
34	35	38	
02	03	06	12
18	19	21	24
26	31	35	

project
Plakate Schwarz/Weiss
Black & White Posters Exhibition poster
Silkscreened in black

client
Willisau Rathaus
Art Gallery
Willisau, Switzerland

design
Niklaus Troxler Design
Niklaus Troxler
Willisau, Switzerland

These two posters demonstrate the versatility inherent in a modular grid. In each, the module size is related to the poster's content.

The New Year poster produced for a silkscreen printer uses a tight modular grid as the basis for its colorful interpretation of the calendar year. The modules represent all the days of the year, organized in twelve columns of thirty-one rows each. Every day of the week is assigned a different color. The uneven mathematical repetition of days, measured against the uniform commencement of each month, creates a randomized pattern of color that simultaneously evokes the cyclical matrix of the calendar and a shower of confetti.

The exhibition poster uses a much larger module as the basis for its composition. The letters forming the exhibition's title are laid out in a 4 x 5 grid of vertically proportioned modules that bleed to the edges of the poster's format—there are no margins. The alternating black and white fields create backgrounds for the individual letters.

The designer "cheats" his grid a little to ensure the legibility of the letters, shifting them upward or sideways to help reveal their forms, but the grid's integrity remains. Overlaps and vibrating juxtapositions of black and white areas introduce detail variation on top of the regular understructure. The dramatic scale of the title gives way to a more focused column of time and date description in the far right column.

structure

Modular grid
with compound
articulations

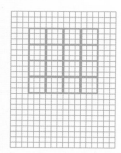

exhibit comparisons

1. RESEARCH

Led by Dr. George Yancopoulos, Regeneron Research Laboratories has generated the array of product candidates that fill our pipeline today. It is comprised of approximately 200 talented and dedicated scientists, including over 65 M.D.'s and/or Ph.D.'s, and is directed by some of the most respected scientists in their fields. We have exciting research programs underway in areas where there are clear market opportunities, including obesity, inflammatory diseases, cancer, asthma, angiogenesis, blood vessel damage and leak, muscle atrophy, liver fibrosis, osteoarthritis, and bone disorders. Certain of these efforts are conducted in partnership with Procter & Gamble as part of our long-term collaboration. We also collaborate with Medarex Inc. to develop monoclonal antibodies as potential drugs.

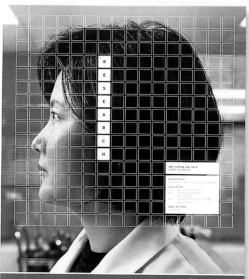

" WHAT EXCITES ME ABOUT WORKING IN THIS LAB?
OUR COLLECTIVE DRIVE TO EXCEL. THIS IS A TEAM. WHEN WE MAKE
A BREAKTHROUGH IN ONE AREA — SAY, DEVELOP A NEW DRUG DISCOVERY
TECHNOLOGY — IT LEADS TO BREAKTHROUGHS IN OTHER AREAS.
WE'RE ALL IN THIS TOGETHER. "

3. CLINICAL TRIALS

We ended 2000 with product candidates in clinical development addressing a variety of unmet medical needs, including AXOKINE®, which is expected to advance into a Phase III trial for severe obesity later this year, and our IL-1 Trap, which is in a Phase I trial for rheumatoid arthritis. We plan to introduce three more drugs into the clinic in 2001 — a pegylated form of AXOKINE for severe obesity, our VEGF Trap for cancer and/or related conditions, and our IL-4/13 Trap for asthma. As these product candidates enter the clinic, responsibility for trial design and oversight falls to the company's clinical development and regulatory groups whose members have the insight and experience necessary to move drugs into human clinical trials and through the drug approval process.

" OUR RESEARCH DISCOVERIES ARE ENTERING THE CLINIC AT A PACE
NEVER SEEN BEFORE AT REGENERON. OVER THE NEXT YEAR, WE EXPECT
TO HAVE ONGOING CLINICAL TRIALS INVOLVING FIVE OR MORE POTENTIAL
DRUGS — AND THESE DRUGS WILL ADDRESS MAJOR DISEASES LIKE
OBESITY, RHEUMATOID ARTHRITIS, CANCER, AND ASTHMA. "

project
Annual Report 2001
Perfect-bound book
Paper cover
Offset lithography

client
Regeneron
Pharmaceutical research
and development
Tarrytown, NY

design
Ideas on Purpose
Darren Namaye
New York, NY

photography
Horatio Salinas
New York, NY

SELECT RESEARCH

In an unusual deviation from regular modular grids, where the same module governs every page regardless of the information being presented, this small-format annual report uses three separate articulations of a modular grid, each with its own module proportion based on the underlying module proportion. The individual grids are tailored to specific sections or types of display. Over several sections, the alternation of individual grids repeats, lending a comfortable cadence to the spreads.

A 6 X 8 module grid on left hand-pages during the first section displays corporate environment and structures a paragraph of text below. The top and side margins are defined by the module width; the bottom margin is a half-module deep.

In contrast, the right-hand page uses the base module grid. The grid is visible as an overlay on the photograph. This at first seems decorative, but the grid is used to organize thematic information like a puzzle board, as well as information below it, and so reveals itself to be structural. The smaller module against the close-up face image communicates greater depth of focus, from environment to person to job function. Corporate officers' statements and management discussion uses the first grid structure.

Another module size defines the grid for the financial section, separated from the conceptual section through the use of a contrasting colored paper.

structure

Modified
column grid

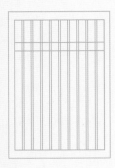

exhibit comparisons

project
Publication system
Book catalogues
Perfect-bound A4 books
Offset lithography

client
Laurence King Publishing
Publishers
London, England

design
Frost Design
Vince Frost
London, England

This quarterly publication promoting a publisher's catalog of offerings is designed using an unusual grid of 1-centimeter vertical divisions with two distinct flowlines, both at the top of the page. Each page in a spread is devoted to the display of a single book. The vertical center line of the page is used as a consistent orientation point for the book's publication information and is flush left from the line and hanging from the first of the flowlines. A narrow horizontal band is defined by the space between the book's information and the beginning of the descriptive text. That text hangs from the second flowline, which also establishes the location of the page marker to the far right. Within the narrow horizontal band, the book's title—in a larger and bolder weight of the same sans serif face used for running text—is stacked upward from the lower flowline line by line as needed. The multiple vertical divisions, meanwhile, allow the designer to introduce rhythm and movement to the text by shifting the paragraph alignment back and forth. Sometimes this shift accommodates the format of the book cover that is shown and other times it is an optical response to the dynamics of the other elements in the spread. The left flush of the paragraph always returns to an alignment with the informa-tion hanging at the top to give resolution to the page.

structure
Modular grid

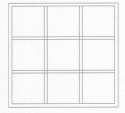

exhibit comparisons

A simple yet clever use of a large-scale grid creates a brochure with staying power. The square format of the folded brochure becomes the governing module for photographs and information as it expands through unfolding. Each time a panel is opened, new components of the overall message are revealed. The simple sequence makes the message clear. When the brochure is completely unfolded, a small poster of flat-color modules and cropped photographs remains as a simple branding message.

project
Track Nine
Foldout brochure/poster
Offset lithography

client
Track Nine
Audio recording and
production studios
New York, NY

design
Level Design
Jennifer Bernstein [AD]
Nicholas Hubbard
New York, NY

structure

Proportional modular grid

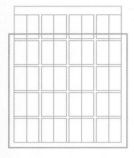

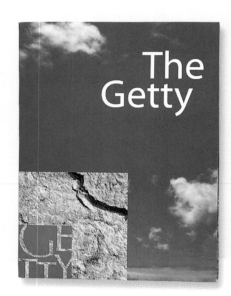

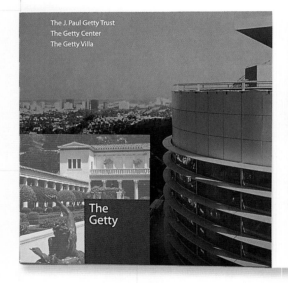

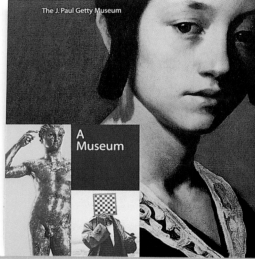

Based on a square logo (which refers to relevant architectural details), this media kit and literature system use a modular grid to accommodate information for five separate educational and research entities bearing the Getty name.

The square module is always derived from a measure that is a quarter width of a given format, helping to partition and unify disparate types of competing images—paintings, sculpture, calligraphy, architecture—both formally and conceptually, across numerous formats.

This unification happens because of the way the square housing of each image neutralizes its individual character (to a certain extent); the brain is made to understand them as relating to each other because they are inside squares. The square housing also helps reinforce the relationship of these images to the Getty brand itself: they become the many different things that are brought together by the institution for research and exhibition.

project
Print collateral system
Media kit folders and
informational brochure
Offset lithography

client
Getty Research Institute
Art and art historical
research and museums
Los Angeles, CA

design
Frankfurt Balkind
Aubrey Balkind [CD]
Kent Hunter [CD]
Todd St. John
New York, NY

The squares are a simple visual device that can
be combined into spatial zones or sequenced in
scale to create kinetic effects when pages are
turned or folders are opened. The brochure folds
neatly in half to a small size without disturbing
the imagery because the fold falls on a grid line.

structure

Column grid

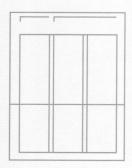

exhibit comparisons

02	05	08	12
14	18	22	26
28	33	37	
04	05	07	09
10	13	15	16
24	27	30	31
36			

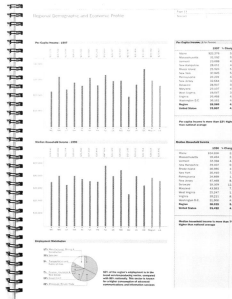

project
Investor's Reference Guide
Informational brochure
Tab-divided, spiral-bound book with two weights of paper stock
Offset lithography

client
Bell Atlantic Company
Public telecommunications services
New York, NY

design
Allemann, Almquist + Jones
Hans U. Alleman [CD]
Philadelphia, PA

A strong, three-column grid with carefully considered margin and column-gutter proportions creates accessibility for a large volume of complex information. The text block of three columns hangs from a more-narrow margin at top, reducing the optical effect of "gravity" and helping the reader to calmly digest the multitude of charts, diagrams, and subheaded text paragraphs within the body of the document. Careful attention to type sizes, interline spacing, and margin relationships keeps the information integrated, yet distinct, without cluttering.

Most pages are divided into three distinct zones: a top band, defined by two flowlines, calls out section number, section title and page number; the inside two columns are used as a single wide column for introductory statements and running text; and the outer column is reserved for diagrams, charts and maps.

The wide variety of information creates constant change in the layout of pages, even though the grid is so regular.

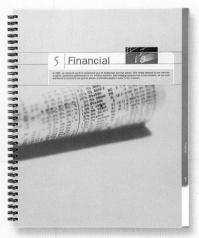

The tab section-dividers adhere to their own simple grid, which treats information consistently in style and placement. Variation is introduced through changes in image and color.

structure

Compound column
and hierarchical grid

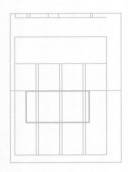

exhibit comparisons

Codified headlines, silhouetted line drawings, and masked-out corporate activity provide intrigue in this annual report for Gartner, a technology consultant to leading technology companies. The secretive nature of the company's client relationships, conveyed in the austere illustrations and censored documents, is given greater tension through the use of a rigorous compound column grid. One-, two-, and four-column page structures alternate to accommodate conceptual texts, stark illustrations in vast white space, complex charts, and consolidated financial information.

project
Annual Report
Perfect-bound book
Offset lithography

client
Gartner Group
Electronic data security
systems
Stamford, CT

design
Cahan+Associates
San Francisco, CA

photography
Lars Tunbjork
Steven Algren
Catherine Ledner
San Francisco, CA

Mirrored two-column text blocks create a deep margin for the gutter and bring the column edges close to the edge of the format, creating extra tension. In other spreads, the gutter proportions are swapped; this dramatic change allows the designer to vary the structure of the layout and introduce a decisive sense of uncertainty that aids in the communication of the content.

The single paragraph of text for the case studies defines the one-column grid. Its dramatic highlighting in yellow separates it from the linear illustration that floats ominously in the remainder of the spread. Four columns help to control listing information, as well as groupings of charts and financial data.

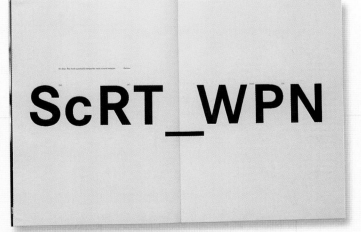

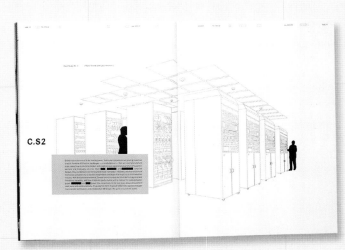

structure
Modular grid

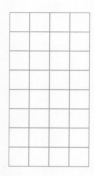

exhibit comparisons

03	04	06	07
09	10	13	16
17	19	22	24
25	27	29	30
35	38		
02	03	05	06
12	18	19	21
24	26	30	31
35			

project
**Arthur Kornberg,
Nobel Laureate**
Exhibition installation

*Steel armiture
Modular pre-printed panels*

client
**University of Rochester
Medical Center**
Graduate medical school

Rochester, NY

design
Poulin + Morris
L. Richard Poulin
Jonathan Posnett

New York, NY

This simply constructed traveling exhibition about a Nobel Prize winner's life balances the studied rigor of a square-module grid with gracefully curved panels and details of bright color. The grid is an enlarged modular grid, without interstices between the modules. Text and images relating the story of Arthur Kornberg's life are arranged around the grid: interlocking, changing horizontal and vertical stress, moving over and under individual modules but always adhering to it.

The modular grid, specifically, allows numerous shaped images to integrate seamlessly without having to resort to translucency or montage effects that might not reproduce well at exhibition-sized scale. Some elements are two modules high by three wide, whereas some are two modules square. Clever shifts in alignment and insets of flat color and type against textural backgrounds create a smooth, unbroken continuum of image and words from the beginning panel to the last.

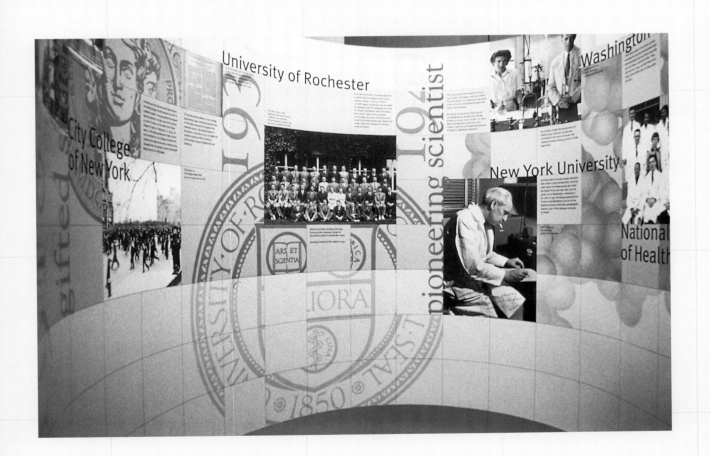

structure
Modified column grid

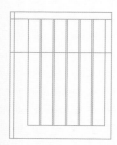

exhibit comparisons

De techniek
van de
Nederlandse
boek-
illustratie
in de
19e eeuw

project
Kerstnummer Grafisch Nederland
Promotional book

Offset lithography with foil stamped cover, die-cuts and tip-ins

client
KVGO
Dutch Royal Foundation of Graphic Enterprises
Amsterdam, Netherlands

design
Una (Amsterdam) Designers
Hans Bockting
Will de l'Ecluse
Amsterdam, Netherlands

KVGO annually publishes a book to promote its members' activities and highlight the skills of graphic artists in general. The 1995 edition is about the technique of Dutch book illustration in the nineteen century. For optimal presentation of the various techniques, UNA used foldouts, inserts, and die cuts, as well as a wide range of paper stock. The text and images are placed on an intricate, six-column modular grid with ten modules vertically. Each module is divided in half vertically, and all text baselines, from the top of the page, are available as hanglines should the need arise.

This grid is designed to accommodate numerous, unusual nonstandard illustration formats, which are presented wherever they fit, so long as they align with the grid; they're permitted to float behind or interfere with the regular double-column of running text, and often straddle the gutter.

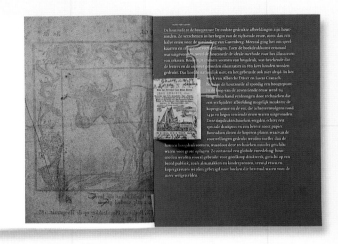

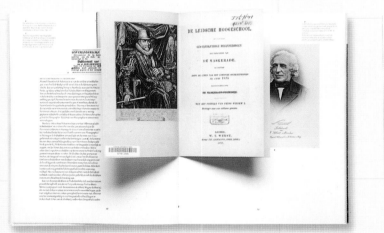

The home starting point for captions is a secondary outer margin that is mirrored from left to right pages. The smaller type size and column width for the captions correspond to the single-width column defined by the module.

Inserts of varying sizes and paper stocks are tipped in and do not necessarily adhere to the grid. This unexpected violation is sometimes applied to the illustrations that are actually printed on the main text page. The interaction between these trompe-l'oeil images and the three-dimensional pop-ups creates a rich dimensionality.

structure
Modified
manuscript grid

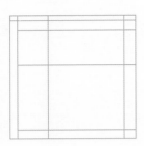

exhibit comparisons

01	05	12	21
01	13	27	30
31	36	37	

project
Annual report
Perfect bound book with double spine, printed offset lithography with die-cuts

client
Lang & Schwarz Wertpapierhandel AG
Financial Services
Dusseldorf, Germany

design
In(corporate Communication + Design GmbH
Karsten Unterberger
Berlin, Germany

A square format for this financial services company's annual report plays off the modular nature of squares. Using a simple manuscript grid with wide margins that are sometimes used for notations or call outs, the designers have split the open double square for one important purpose: Each side carries the same information, the left running in German and the right in English.

The majority of the book is given to management discussion of financial matters and business initiatives, but colorful, conceptual section dividers showcase customer interaction with the company, acting as positioning statements and welcome interludes between long sections of figures and text. Their surreal photographic compositions are understated and almost devoid of human imagery, yet a kind of uncomfortable intimacy pervades them.

Inserted into a pocket inside the front cover are a series of quad-folded financial statements. Each is two-sided and displays the same data in German and English for a quick reference of the complex material buried inside the report.

exhibit comparisons

03	06	07	09
10	13	17	19
22	24	25	27
29	30	35	37
02	03	06	12
18	19	21	24
26	30	31	

VIBRATO
Naming, Inc.

Who we are
How we create vibrant names
Why vibrant?
Solutions
Collaborations
Clients speak
Process
Meet Vibrato
Position papers
Contact

When your brand can
inspire and persuade
the people who are
vital to your success,
you can compete.

We help companies become
more valuable by creating
vibrant brand names for global
businesses, products, and
services. Names that both resound above
the marketplace uproar and resonate with the
constituencies among your audience—from
your target market, current employees, potential
recruits, industry press, to your prospective
investors and merger partners.

This Web site is organized around a simple modular grid. The modules are
horizontally stressed, echoing the landscape orientation of the browser
window and their organization into five columns and four rows. The top
row generally remains blank, acting as a holding area for the branding
message and as a way of separating the page content from the browser
navigation. In the second row, the first two modules, beginning at the left,
are reserved for the primary navigation. A restrained color change indicates
selection and location within the site. The information that has been
selected is given prominence in the central two columns, with supplemental
information appearing in a highlighted module to the left or right. Links
within the central row call up more specific information in the bottom
rows, which are sometimes displayed as columns and sometimes as
individual modules.

project
www.vibratonaming.com
Internet site
Flash version 5.0

client
Vibrato
Corporate naming and
marketing strategy
Malibu, CA

design
Intersection Studio
San Francisco, CA

VIBRATO
Naming, Inc.

Who we are
How we create vibrant names
Why vibrant?
Solutions
Collaborations
Clients speak
Process
Meet Vibrato
Position papers
Contact

Why Vibrant?

A vibrant brand name **resounds** to:

- Assert your differential advantage
- Capture attention
- Rankle your competition
- Begin building recognition
- Be unquestionably memorable

Because mindshare
drives marketshare

And **resonates** to:

- Shoulder as much of your marketing burden as possible
- Initiate a meaningful, relevant, and persuasive relationship
  with your audience
- Reflect the voice, spirit, and values of your offering
- Set appropriate expectations, allowing for the evolution
  of your offering, technology, and social mores
- Be worth remembering

VIBRATO
Naming, Inc.

Who we are
How we create vibrant names
Why vibrant?
Solutions
Collaborations
Clients speak
Process
Meet Vibrato
Position papers
Contact

Solutions

Re-Naming
Launches
Retail
  Products
Film Titles
Taglines
Nomenclature

As You Like It	Berried Treasures	Dex	Go Figure
		Challenge: The New Yellow Pages	
		Positioning: Easy access to information you need	
LEGENDairy	Nectar Imperial		*Strategy by Dietenbach Elkins

VIBRATO
Naming, Inc.

Who we are
How we create vibrant names
Why vibrant?
Solutions
Collaborations
Clients speak
Process
Meet Vibrato
Position papers
Contact

Process

1. Situation, Intent, and Opportunity Study
2. Name Creation: NomenCulture™
3. Report Development
4. Client Decision

Our process
empowers us to
deliver vibrant
solutions.

First Wave Name Generation

- For each facet of each naming path, explore literal and symbolic lexicons
- Harvest a new lexicon: words and morphemes
- Cross-pollinate words, morphemes and ideas
- Self-refine and recommend naming candidates with rationale using client's strategic
  objectives and Vibrato's creative standards
- Collate into a first wave master list

Review/Refinements and Second Wave by Senior Team

- Review and score first wave master list
- Explore literal and symbolic lexicons with tighter focus
- Cross-pollinate and self-refine
- Recommend naming candidates with rationale
- Submit and collate with first wave master list into a final master list

VIBRATO
Naming, Inc.

Who we are
How we create vibrant names
Why vibrant?
Solutions
Collaborations
Clients speak
Process
Meet Vibrato
Position papers
Contact

Clients Speak

BrandNew Consulting
Frontera Corporation
Hilton & DoubleTree Hotels
H.P. Hood
Jettis
  Lexis-Nexis
Protocol
siegelgale
Soutellis Studio
St. Aubyn
Wechsler Ross & Partners

"The thoroughness of her process, along with her creative energy, led to
a winning product name every time. Meredith brings skill and artistry to
every project."

Tisha Gray, Marketing Director
Lexis-Nexis

Format-dependent modular grid

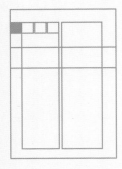

exhibit comparisons

In this rigorously disciplined stationery system for a multinational apparel manufacturer, a strict modular grid helps coordinate internal company communication documents across three continents. The module that orders the document structures is the company's logo itself. The proportion of the red square changes in each format, but its size in a given format determines the placement of all typographic material therein. By setting up specific, related column structures in all of the printed materials, the modular grid helps order multiple addresses and complex forms for a coherent, recognizable brand image.

project
Corporate identity
Stationery system
Offset lithography and spot engraving

client
DZ Group
Apparel manufacturers
*New York, NY
Los Angeles, CA*

*Shanghai and Hong Kong,
People's Republic of China*

design
Paone Design Associates
Gregory Paone
Philadelphia, PA

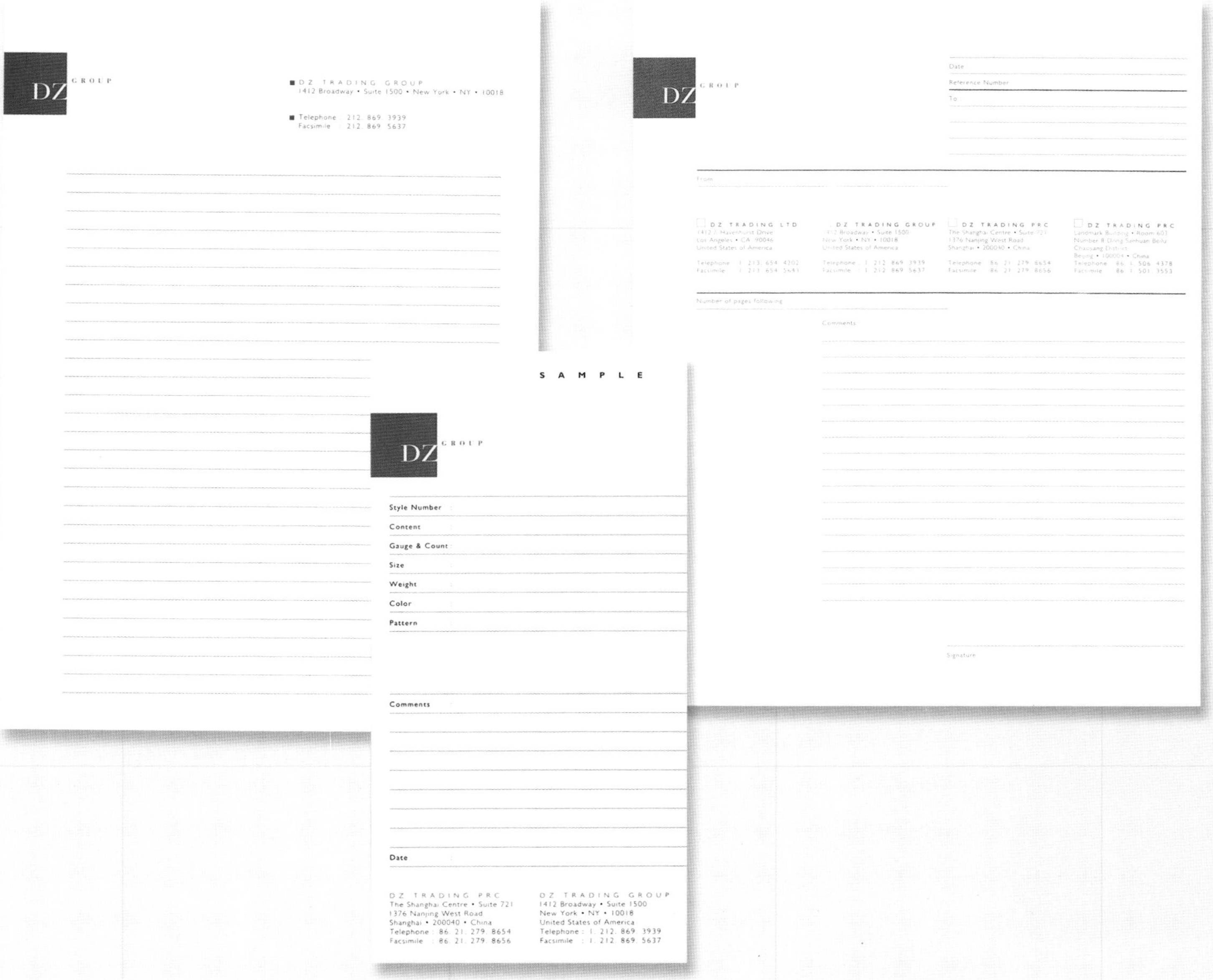

structure

Column grid

exhibit comparisons

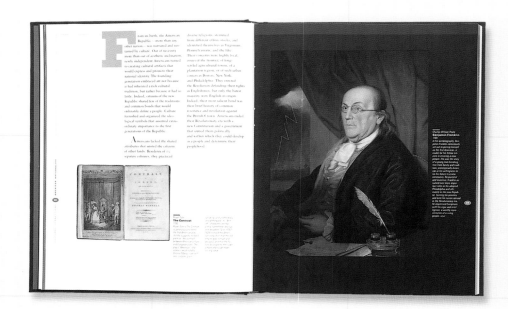

project
Cultural Connections
Book
Casebound with jacket
Offset lithography

client
Temple University Press
Academic publishers
Philadelphia, PA

design
Katz Wheeler
Joel Katz [AD]
Philadelphia, PA

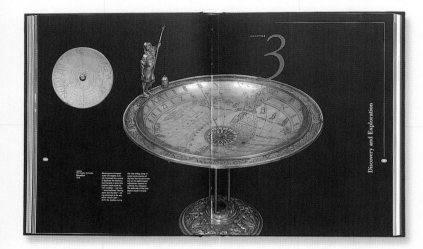

A six-column grid supplied the variety needed to encompass an enormous variety of artifacts, descriptions, and listings for this hardcover book on the museums and libraries of Philadelphia and the Delaware Valley.

For essays and their supporting images in the book's first section, the six columns are used as three. Running text hangs from a single flowline near the top of the page, starting and ending with a complete paragraph. Each spread is informationally independent: only images referred to in the text on that spread are shown. The tremendous flexibility inherent in the column grid allows the designers to vary the layouts to accommodate unusually-shaped artifacts, but the hangline and natural ending depths of the text give a unified quality to the information.

Captions occupy a single, narrow column and can be placed in close proximity to the image they notate; the precision of the six-column grid ensures they always align with it, regardless of where they must be placed.

In the listing of institutions that makes up the book's second major section, this text structure is even more useful; each institution's listing, no matter how involved, is available at a glance. Captions in this section occupy a single column between two double-wide text columns. Each width is suited to the respective type size and function of the information.

structure

Modular grid

Japanese designer Igarashi's signature three-dimensional letterform sculptures fill a modular grid in this exhibition poster. The grid is used to provide distinct components of information—venue, date and time, event sponsor—and as a convenient way to group dozens of photographs of the letter sculptures. Thoughtful placement of individual images sets up optical rhythms within the rows and columns of square snapshots, almost like the storyboard of a film sequence.

exhibit comparisons

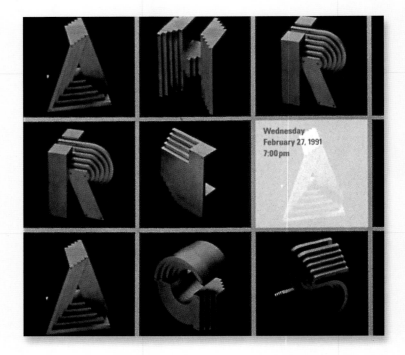

Wednesday
February 27, 1991
7:00 pm

The translucent white modules separate from the background to draw attention to the information, and their asymmetric arrangement heightens the sense of movement within the format.

project
Takenobu Igarashi
Exhibition/lecture poster
*Offset lithography,
two colors*

client
AIGA
American Institute of
Graphic Arts,
New York Chapter
New York, NY

design
Poulin + Morris
L. Richard Poulin
New York, NY

photography
Takenobu Igarashi
Tokyo, Japan

structure
Compound modular and hierarchical grid

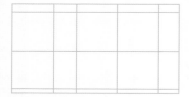

exhibit comparisons

Visitors to the Books of Hope site, a subsection of Brittanica.com, can interact with some of the most important thinkers in the world, participate in discussions, view biographies, and peruse an extensive image gallery. A hierarchical grid houses the various areas and incorporates a number of interactive tools developed specifically for the site: timelines, galleries, and a forum in which users can respond to contributors' essays.

project
www.brittanica.com/
booksofhope/
Internet site
DHTML and Java Script

client
Brittanica, Inc.
Publishers
Chicago, IL

design
MetaDesign SF
San Francisco, CA

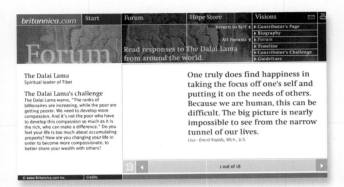

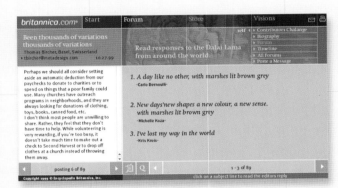

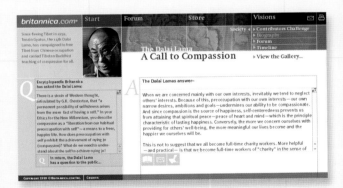

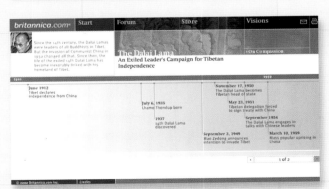

The hierarchy is divided into four major areas: a branded navigational bar relating to Brittanica.com; a navigational area housed in modules that expand or collapse as needed; a left-hand column that acts as a lead-in or informational addendum to the primary content; and the primary content area, which houses timelines, essays, and biographies.

Each hierarchical area assumes importance or diminishes in importance depending on where the user is located within the site; careful attention to type sizes and luminosity differences between grid areas helps some information recede when needed. The most important information in a particular screen comes forward clearly.

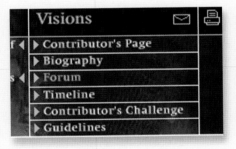

The modular nature of the structure becomes evident in the interface details such as markers, pagination icons, and menus.

structure
Modified
manuscript grid

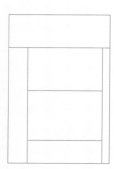

exhibit comparisons

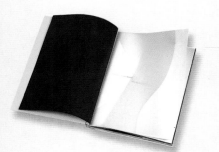

philosophy

"Praise the virtues of the earth which nurture new life and bring forth
significant values."
— Ekikyo-Konka
(from *A Book of Divination Concerning the Virtues of the Empress*)

This Japanese philosophy is the source of the name Shiseido. We trust that
our success will always come from creating innovative products that bring
greater beauty and harmony to people's personal lives.

philosophy

As a company, we are unified by five simple principles. They help us all
work toward a common vision, and they help us each take uncommon
pride in our work.

Quality above all We pursue absolute excellence in everything we create

Co-existence and Co-prosperity Everyone associated with Shiseido must
benefit in a significant way

Respect for others We seek to understand our customers' needs, and those
needs guide our product development

Stability We respect the company's past achievements, and choose intelligent
goals for the future

Sincerity Sincerity, loyalty and honesty are our fundamental principles
of business

savor   because it will be gone tomorrow

Practicing this philosophy for well over a century, Shiseido has developed as
a truly contemporary company, consistently on the leading edge of wellness
and beauty. It is a source of great pride to us that our governing philosophy
has brought such rewards.

project
Beauty
Product promotional book
Casebound book
Embossed cover, heavy rag
printmaking paper
Text printed offset on
coated stock and vellum

client
Shiseido Cosmetics
Cosmetics manufacturer
Tokyo, Japan

design
Tolleson Design
Steve Tolleson [AD]
John Barretto
San Francisco, CA

photography
Thomas Arledge
Morley Baer
Chip Forelli
Anthony Gordon
Sal Graceffa
David Martinez
Glen McClure
David Peterson
Robert Sebree

illustration
Graphistock Stock
Image Bank Stock
Photonica Stock

A center-axis grid and translucent papers give restrained definition to the manuscript structure used for this promotional book. Relatively wide lateral margins and an especially deep head margin set the primary text block low on the page and give it comfortable room within the small format. A strong horizon links photographic spreads containing a single line of type to the justified blocks of text with a vertical axis.

See-through vellum is printed in sheets twice the width of the regular text pages so that it can be folded and bound with its leading edge out. Paragraphs of text printed on both sides of the folded vellum are visible; distinct flowlines designate areas for these corresponding areas of text so they don't overlap each other from side to side; instead they step out of the way.

Foreground and background text engage in subtle shifts of alignment with the photographic images on the pages before and underneath. The sense of continuity between the text and contrasting types of images—color/black-and-white, product/figure, figure/landscape— is maintained though the consistency of the grid's simplicity.

structure

**Proportionally
integrated column
and modular grids**

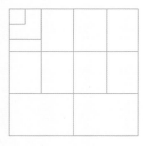

exhibit comparisons

jersey city
museum

350 Montgomery Street, Jersey City, NJ 07302

Anne DeVivo DeMesa
Development Officer
201.413.0303 x3108, 201.413.9922 fax
ademesa@jerseycitymuseum.org

project
Corporate identity
Stationery, print collateral,
and signage applications

*Offset lithography and
large-format plotter*

client
Jersey City Museum
Cultural and arts museum
Jersey City, NJ

design
C. Harvey Graphic Design
Catherine Lee
New York, NY

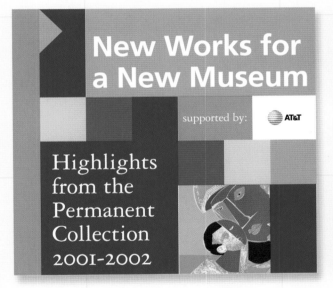

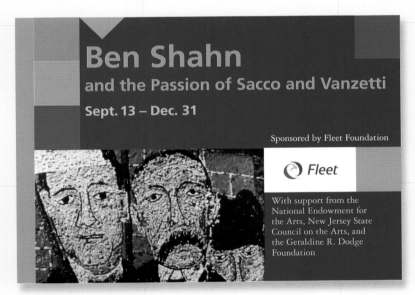

In this identity system, a system of grid types and modular design elements unifies the communication for a cultural institution and provides flexibility for new applications. All of the materials use a grid of columns defined by the format's proportions, rather than a set of predetermined proportions, as is often the case with large-scale identity programs; sometimes two columns are needed, sometimes four. In all cases, a consistent set of flowlines separates the given format in half or into thirds or quarters. The relationship between the columns is allowed to change: in the newsletter, the columns run next to each other for continuous text, but are allowed to break into a half-column width to accommodate captions for images; in the membership brochures, the columns are spaced for the narrow panels of the three-fold format to retain the asymmetry of the margins that characterizes the larger applications. In some instances, the column grid becomes modular and literally articulated as squares of color, as in the exterior exhibition banners. This modularity helps accomplish several goals: it creates a more promotional presentation appropriate to the message's context; it allows the same format to unify drastically different messages and artwork that is being promoted; and it helps to reinforce the architectural source of the museum's logo—the rotated square decorative element from the building's facade. The module shape is also used extensively as a counterpoint to the vertical column and bar structure throughout the informational literature.

Hierarchical grid

exhibit comparisons

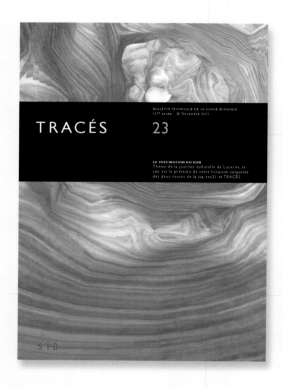

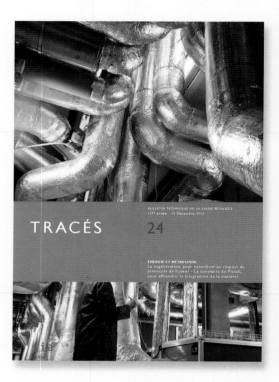

The image material provided for consideration in designing this trade magazine's covers was of low quality; for budgetary reasons no new photography would be possible. As a solution, and to create distinction, the designer implemented a compositional system based on a colored band that holds the masthead, which is able to slide up and down on the cover in response to whatever image is available.

The A4 format is divided first by a square of its width, based on the proportioning of the golden section in classical architecture. The masthead band is equal in height to one-third of that square. Within the band, the information—magazine name, volume number, and contents—is distributed vertically along flowlines that divide the band into quarters and is broken by a vertical division that also corresponds to the golden section. The width of one-quarter of the band establishes the outer margins for typography.

As the band is positioned during the design process, it reveals and obscures different aspects of the background photograph, and it also divides the entire page in harmonious proportions relating to the golden section. The aggressively rigorous geometry of the layout system helps to mask the poor quality of the images and helps create consistency between editions.

project
Masthead & cover system
Tracés magazine
Offset lithography

client
IAS/*Tracés* Magazine
Interior design and
architectural publishers
Eclubens, Switzerland

design
Atelier Poisson
Giorgio Pesce
Lausanne, Switzerland

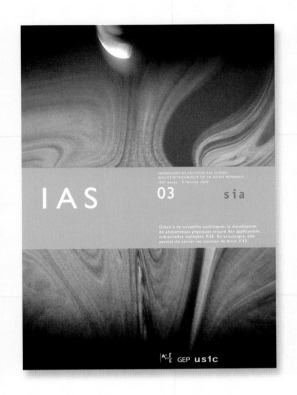

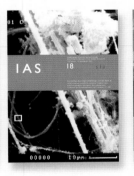

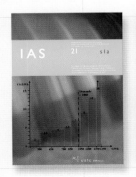

structure

Modular grid

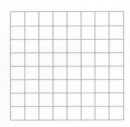

A comfortably proportioned modular grid provides overall branding continuity and endless layout variations for Springer, a publisher of textbooks. The program uses a grid of modules that, unlike other grids of this kind, butt each other like a chessboard. The lack of gutters or margins means that the actual book formats can be configured on the grid for greater consistency, and the gridded image areas always align with each other and with the book's spine and edges.

The schematic shows the publisher's in-house designers a number of options for using the grid to vary the placement of images, type areas, and areas of flat color. Sequences of books in a single subject can be grouped with a single layout, but be given their own identities through color and image variation. Bold scientific materials, as well as more reserved layouts for literature and critical essays, are equally possible.

exhibit comparisons

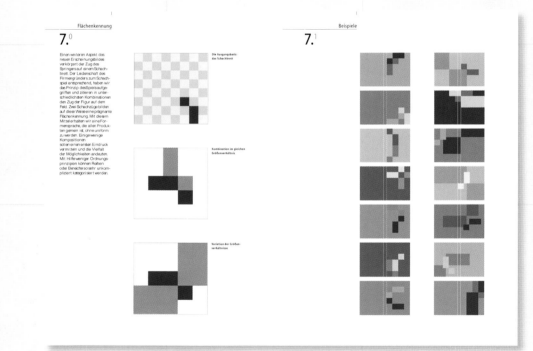

project
Book cover design system
Typographic and color
standards, cover design
application

client
Springer Verlag
Publishers
Berlin, Germany

design
MetaDesign Berlin
Berlin, Germany

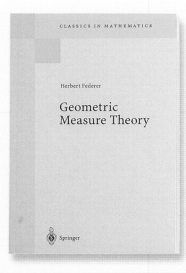

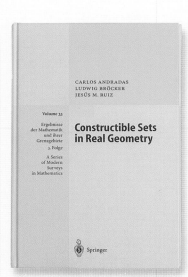

Modular grid

exhibit comparisons

03	06	07	09
10	13	16	17
19	24	27	29
30	35	37	
02	06	07	12
18	19	21	26
28	31	36	

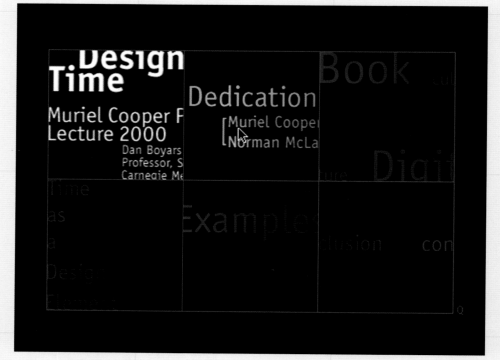

This digital presentation uses animated sequences and navigation through a modular grid to give support to a lecturer. The module is a square, made visible as gray hairline rules. Each module in the main content menu displays specific information and acts as a link to the information when clicked on with a cursor. The module is subdivided to reveal the detailed set of information within it, and each of these subdivisions links to additional information expanding on that selected topic.

An unobtrusive arrow at the left of the module frame permits the lecturer to return to a previous frame. Organizing the naturally dendritic structure of interactive navigation through a grid helps to maintain visual continuity between the various "frames" or "pages;" the number of subdivisions within the viewing area lets the lecturer know their depth in the information structure; and the grid provides a way for the lecturer to seamlessly and spontaneously select a path through the presentation without having to reprogram or reorganize the information.

project
Designing with Time
Digital presentation

school
**Carnegie Mellon
University**
Educational institution
Pittsburgh, PA

design
**Heebok Lee
Daniel Boyarski**
Pittsburgh, PA

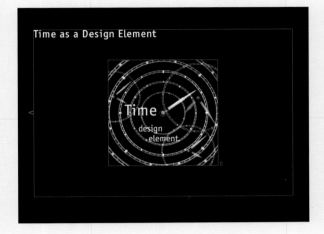

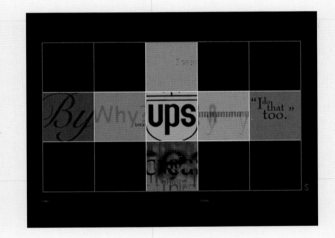

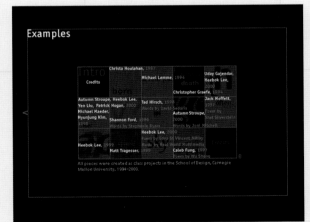

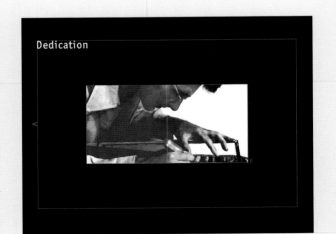

structure

Column grid

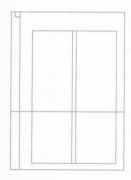

exhibit comparisons

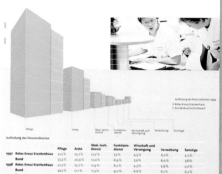

project
Fiscal report
*Perfect-bound book with
kraft paper cover
Text printed offset on
matte-coated stock with
die cutting and plastic
film inserts*

client
Rotes Kreuz Krankenhaus
Red Cross Hospital
Bremen, Germany

design
**In(corporate
Communication + Design
GmbH**
Karsten Unterberger
Berlin, Germany

photography
Thomas Hellmann
Bremen, Germany

Hofmann + Reichelt
Oldenberg, Germany

A conventional, two-column grid is given extra dimensionality in this fiscal report for a Berlin hospital. The wide left margin, which houses an elaborate vertical folio, orients the two primary text columns asymmetrically on the page. Running text for a given section flows from the left-most column until it ends, whether that is within the right-hand column on the left page, or on the right-hand page. Sidebar or illustrative elements flap inward over the second column of the right-hand page as a gatefold, providing elaboration and lifting to reveal additional text or image. Sometimes this flap offers interactive information, such as pop-ups or pull-tabs, or special tipped-in images, such as X-Ray film.

In each spread, the bottom third is divided from the upper part of the page by a hangline that defines an area for graphs, medical diagrams, and financial information. Financial highlights presented toward the back of the report use both columns for width.

structure

Modular grid

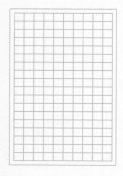

exhibit comparisons

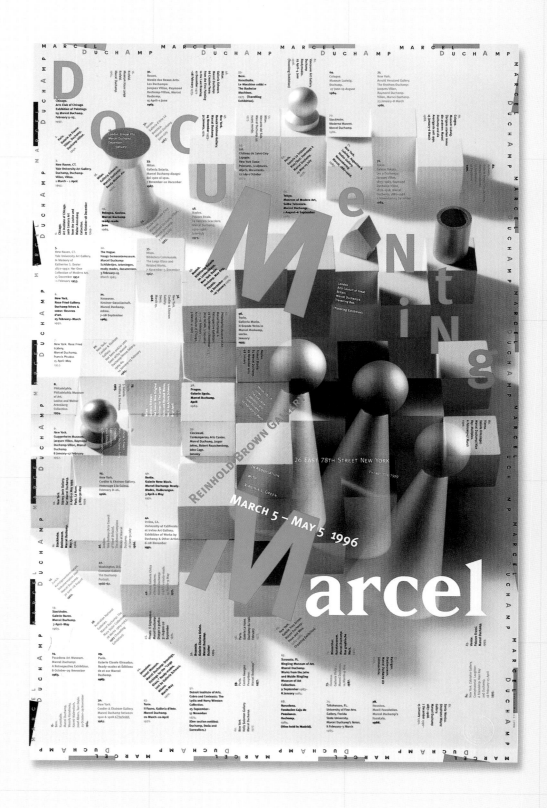

project
Documenting Marcel
Exhibition poster
Silkscreen, two colors

client
Reinhold-Brown Gallery
Art gallery
New York, NY

design
Skolos/Wedell
Canton, MA

photography
Skolos/Wedell
Canton, MA

While this heavily gridded poster displays some characteristics of deconstruction (explored in-depth in the next section, *Breaking the Grid*), its structure is based on a grid inherent in the content of the exhibition it describes—a show commemorating all of Dadaist Marcel Duchamp's eighty-one exhibitions. Duchamp was an avid chess player, and the psychology of chess—its hidden strategies, its structural qualities—played an important role in his artistic pursuits, appearing in paintings and acting as an organizing principle in various word games and constructions.

In this poster, the three-dimensional chessboard of the photograph acts as both a conceptual and literal structure for organizing the type, which details all of the artist's exhibitions during his lifetime.

The play of surface generated by the cubes is sometimes perceived as flat, sometimes as advancing, and sometimes receding. Type on these surfaces interacts with the background of each respective "module" and leads the viewer across the board as though the game is being played—a metaphor for retracing events in the artist's career that he may have found intriguing.

structure

Modified column grid

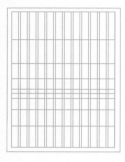

exhibit comparisons

The grid used for this magazine celebrating the human experience and generating awareness about human rights divides the page up into twelve equal columns of 4.5 picas. This mundane structure contrasts with a unique structure of flowlines that emphasizes the horizontal aspect of the spreads; it organizes the material along a pictorial "horizon" line as a reference to human activity on the surface of the Earth.

This horizon line crosses the lower third of the format, and from there the designer based subsequent flowlines on a mathematical progression known as the Fibonacci series. The Fibonacci proportions are found in nature, and here they cause the flowlines to steadily open outward like perspective lines. The hangline for text is therefore relatively low on the page. Text arranged in columns can be shifted along these lines like faults, creating additional optical weight that enhances the lateral movement across the spreads. Sometimes the grid is disregarded for special photographic essays or unusual texts, like those that are spoken or come from letters or notes.

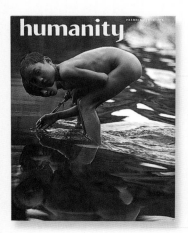

project
Editorial system
Periodical magazine
Offset lithography

client
Humanity Magazine
Providence, RI

design
Thomas Ockerse
Providence, RI

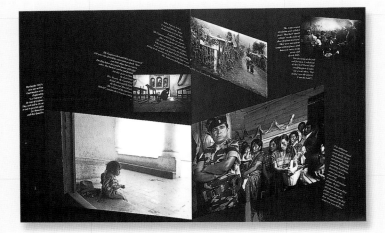

structure
Modular grid

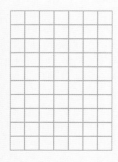

exhibit comparisons

For this trade exhibit of furniture produced by a venerable Italian manufacturer, the designer brings the organizational grid into physical existence. The subtle irony here is that while interior designers use a flat grid to plan a three-dimensional space, the grid is made three-dimensional, and the furniture's "real" presence in this exhibit is represented by a single, iconic chair, set apart from the remaining space on a glass platform exactly three grid-modules square.

The rest of the furniture is displayed as flat photography organized in a three-dimensional plan. As a result, a great deal more furniture can be shown, and the exhibit has a much greater presence because of its unusual approach. Articulating the grid through the use of materials adds a tactile quality and a solidity that imparts a serene order to the space. The modules in the floor are stone blocks; the vertical displays, showcasing the photographs of furniture, are brushed steel planks that have been inserted between the floor blocks. A glass plane under the iconic chair and the floor blocks creates reflection, highlighting the chair's physicality and linking it to the remainder of the grid.

Translucent scrims stretch from the floor in front of walls that have been airbrushed from lighter to darker, and then lit from below, giving the impression that the walls and vertical plinths are floating; despite its apparent rigidity, the grid assumes a light, ethereal quality.

project
Exhibition space
Steel panel flooring
Brushed steel panels
Photographs
Upholstered chair

client
Poltrona Frau
Contract and residential
furnishings
Tolentino, Italy

design
Vignelli Associates
New York, NY

structure

Modular grid (singular and compound)

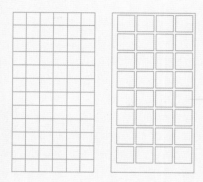

exhibit comparisons

03	06	07	09
10	13	16	17
19	22	24	27
29	35	38	
02	06	09	12
18	19	21	23
26	31	36	

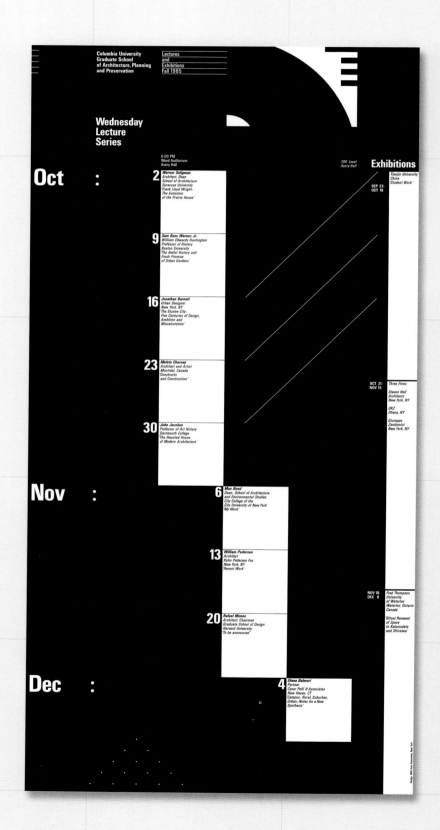

project
Lecture posters
from a continuing series
Offset lithography

client
**Columbia University
School of Architecture**
Educational institution
New York, NY

design
Willi Kunz Associates
New York, NY

Each of these posters, from a long-developed
series for the lecture programs presented by
Columbia University School of Architecture
in New York, is constructed on a modular
grid. The module proportions vary according
to the content specific to each poster, even
though the poster format remains constant.

In the poster at left, the organization of the
lecture calendar is given prominence. Its
modules are clearly visible as individual date
blocks for the lectures, reversed out of the
black field. All the lectures for a given month
occupy their own vertical row; the dates
for the subsequent month are shifted one
module to the right. Graphic details alluding
to architectural forms are used to draw the
disparate areas of the composition together.

In the poster at right, the designer uses the
module more freely, hiding it to a certain
degree behind the optical foreground of
white horizontal bars that order the lecture
information, but revealing it in the widths of
the narrow columns. In fact, several modular
grids are interacting on top of each other,
each lending logic for alignments among the
elements. The sequence of the calendar
moves freely down and across the modules,
given regularity by them but not as directly
related to the module proportions as it is in
the other poster.

**Proportionally
integrated
hierarchical grids**

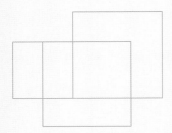

exhibit comparisons

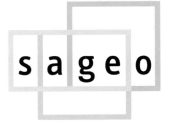

A simple hierarchical grid defines the expression of Sageo's identity. The proportions of the linear logo structure correspond to those of the typography they echo, and this flexibility of proportion carries through to the structuring of the company's print materials. The stationery, for example, reflects this loose grid in line treatments and column areas that depend on the given format's size, shape, and function.

project
Identity system
Stationery applications
and online branding
Offset lithography
DHTML *and Java script*

client
Hewitt Corporation
Health care providers
San Francisco, CA

design
MetaDesign SF
San Francisco, CA

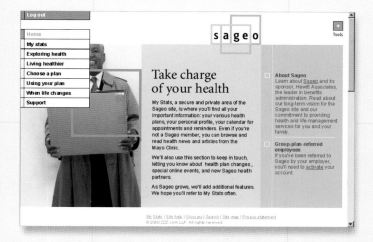

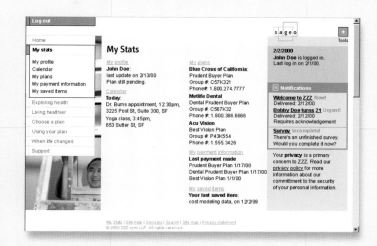

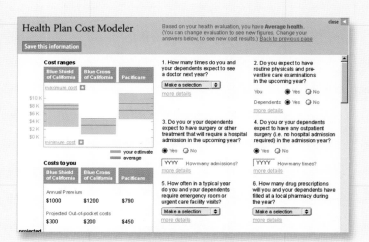

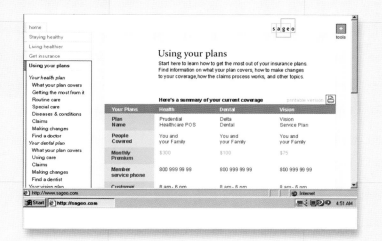

In the letterhead, the area set aside for the body of the letter is integrated with the printed information through linear elements that define the function of these areas. Fields of color on the reverse of the business card correspond to the fields of information on the foreside; similar fields reiterate the logo structure on the cover of the folder.

MetaDesign's solution for the Sageo core identity was extended into the interaction design for the Web site. The simple modular structure is flexible and is sometimes "violated" by a hierarchical grid if the informational needs of a particular screen demand it.

A database of custom photography characterized by a straightforward but quirky snapshot style works into print and online content areas. The photographs strive for a kind of immediacy that reflects real people and real lives, essential elements of the Sageo brand that are wrapped in a comfortable unifying structure.

structure
Hierarchical grid

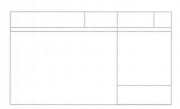

exhibit comparisons

project
www.princetonart.org
Internet site
DHTML and Java Script
© 2002 Princeton University
Art Museum

client
**Princeton University
Museum of Art**
Educational institution
Princeton, NJ

design
Swim Design
Washington, DC

A simple hierarchical grid effectively organizes this art museum's online presence. In what has become a standard grid-based approach for navigating complex information, a horizontal band at the top of the site colorfully distinguishes itself from the content it governs below, which is divided into two distinct areas: a text area and an area for decorative illustration. The division just below the primary navigational area, which lists the most important topics to be covered in the site, expands to list the secondary navigation, or B-levels, corresponding to the main topic, or A-level, that has been selected. Each of these B-level links, when selected, may open a listing of C-level links immediately below.

structure

**Dimensional
column grid**

exhibit comparisons

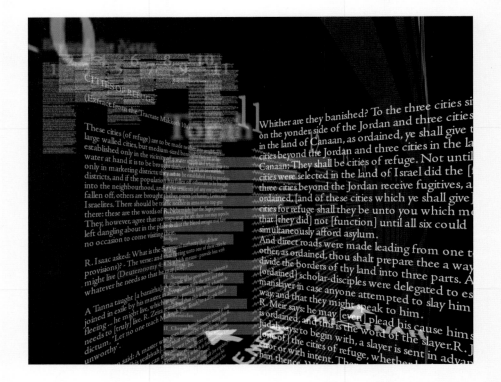

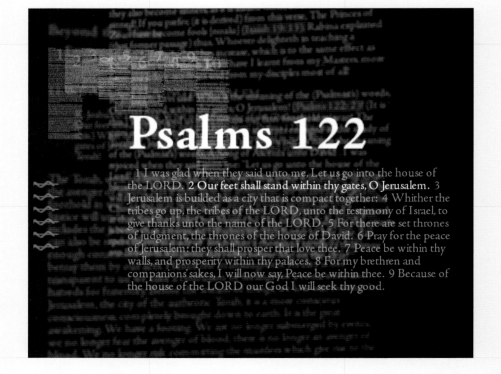

project
The Talmud Project
Dynamic text interface
*Proprietary interactive
digital interface*
© 1999 David Small

client
MIT Media Lab
Educational institution
Cambridge, MA

design
Small Design Firm, Inc.
David Small
Cambridge, MA

Relatively ordinary columns of serif type form the basis of this complex digital information system that combines passages of the Talmud and the Torah, translated into English and French. By turning dials that correspond to different, but related, aspects of the texts, viewers are able to zoom in to specific passages and interactively cross-reference them with related texts in the database. The dials rotate the text columns in virtual space, with each axis around the column linking to other texts or to its translation in the other language. The distribution of the text across the columns changes depending on which dials are selected and, therefore, which aspect of the text is called into view. The grid in this information system allows thousands of pages to be interconnected and accessible within seconds.

structure
Hierarchical grid

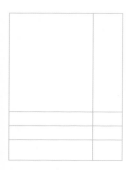

exhibit comparisons

the second book of moses, called

exodus

with an introduction by | david grossman

A grid-based set of proportions, mathematically derived from the width of these small-format Biblical extracts, provides a clean, simple structure for their titling. The depth of the first hangline, for the title itself, is the square of the book's width. The secondary information is given specific position, respective of its place in the hierarchy (subtitle, Biblical notation, author, translator). The use of a structural underline and linear-rule bracket for separation of elements in this area lends contrast to the mysterious photography, as well as a more modern sensibility.

project
The Pocket Canons
Book cover design system
Perfect-bound books
Offset lithography

client
Canongate Books, Ltd.
Publishers
London, England

design
Pentagram UK
Angus Hyland
London, England

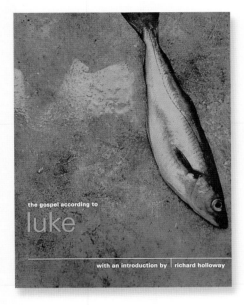

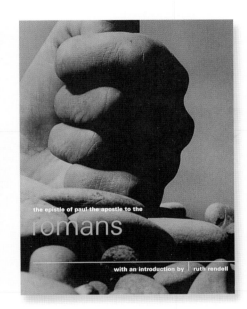

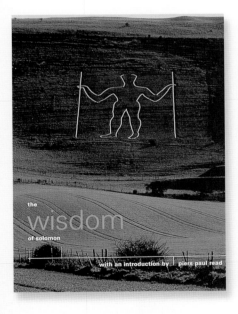

structure

Hierarchic modular grid

project
Embarcadero Center
Architectural signage and
way-finding system

*Freestanding and wall-
mounted steel modular
panels*

client
Embarcadero Center
Shopping and office
complex
San Francisco, CA

design
Poulin + Morris
L. Richard Poulin
New York, NY

The modular grid that organizes this branded public signage system extends from mere layout into the third dimension: the square units are physically modular, meaning that the square base unit can be used singly or combined with others to create freestanding navigational kiosks of any size or complexity. Each module within a kiosk assumes a distinct hierarchical function, and the order of the modules from top to bottom within a kiosk is based on the informational need of the viewer at that juncture within the space. The top module, for example, locates the viewer within a specific building of the shopping complex. The second module in the kiosk provides closest point-of-use information, allowing the viewer to locate what is nearest the kiosk first.

Single-module signs reinforce location and connect the branding directly to the architecture, fitting against walls and echoing the square units of the building's stone surfaces.

structure

Compound grid
(hierarchical, column,
manuscript)

The multiple components of the grid in this intimate, lively annual report seem at odds with its simplistic appearance. The primary grid (which is hierarchical), on closer inspection, gives order to the conceptual verbal principle that governs the report's presentation.

...replaces these things. It makes them more useful. More powerful. More likely to make a difference in your life. General Magic is already creating voice-enabled services that use magicTalk. The first one is called Portico™: a virtual digital assistant who can answer the phone right away whenever y...

exhibit comparisons

The idea of voice-data connection between individuals across the world, through the use of the client company's technology, is the basis for the book's construction. The accordion-fold offers a continuous unbroken format that allows the copy to travel in one long line from end to end.

project
Annual report
*Accordion-folded sheet
with paperboard slipcase
Offset lithography*

client
General Magic
Digital-communications
software developers
Sunnyvale, CA

design
Cahan & Associates
San Francisco, CA

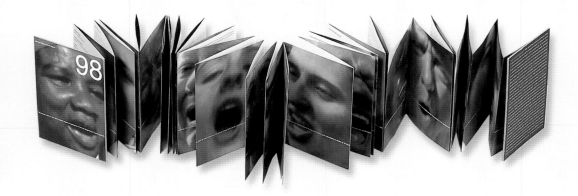

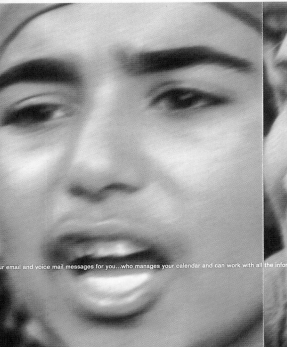

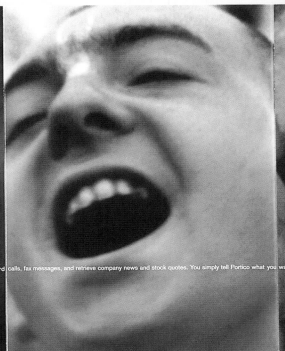

ur email and voice mail messages for you...who manages your calendar and can work with all the information in your address book. Portico also follows your instructions to screen or forward calls, fax messages, and retrieve company news and stock quotes. You simply tell Portico what you want

The placement of that single line is conceptual: it flows across the mouths of all the face photographs that make up the panels of the book. Its precise placement, however, creates a visual structure that locks the format to the content: The line of text divides each panel into a square and a rectangle. In this case, the grid has no margins, and its proportions govern the placement of the faces.

On the reverse, the financial data adheres to a manuscript grid with a text block that is almost the width of the format, in a gesture that echoes the direct contact with the format edge that the grid has on the front side. A narrow column structure is defined by the manuscript text block, encompassing tabular financial data.

structure
Column grid

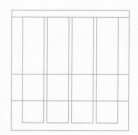

exhibit comparisons

02	05	08	11
12	14	18	22
26	28	33	
04	05	07	09
10	13	15	16
23	24	30	36

looking ahead

Over the next five years, we seek to animate our vision for East Harlem through a set of mutually reinforcing initiatives: housing development, property acquisition, property management, commercial development, community building, capacity building, and strengthening our financial resource

property
acquisition

goal:
300
additional units

HOPE
campaign
the campaign
for hope community

HOPE

Dramatically varied use of a rigorous four-column grid lends a sense of vitality, growth, and optimism to this brochure. The regularity of the grid, however, conveys stability—incredibly important for the client in securing funding from the potential investors to whom the brochure is directed.

project
Hope Campaign
Capital investment
marketing brochure

Saddle-stitched booklet
Offset lithography

client
Hope Community, Inc.
Not-for-profit urban-
property development
New York, NY

design
C. Harvey Graphic Design
Catherine Lee
New York, NY

Major sections are characterized by these varied treatments. A section that focuses on the client organization's accomplishments balances a full-bleed photograph against supporting charts and text. Large-scale typography shifts slightly off the column alignments, reinforced by architecturally inspired blocks of color, to increase a sense of movement and space. Paragraphs of particular importance are separted out from the running text and allowed to span two or three columns. In some instances, photographs are given the same privilege while the text assumes a more rigorous articulation of the columns.

In the section that outlines the client company's current capital campaign, the columns are used more rigorously. Two strong flowlines create a place for important concepts to dominate each page: a headline describing specific types of grants, and the body-text hangline to which is aligned the capital goal figure. These flowlines provide visual continuity to the section, but also give the reader a cue to the most important information on the page.

structure

Dimensional modular grid

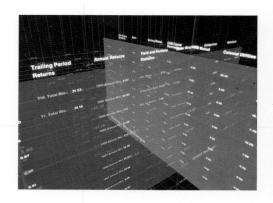

The premise of this pioneering digital interface, produced for a media and design conference, is to add dimension to text information for greater accessibility, as well as to facilitate the connection of related components using a spatial model. It was envisioned that the text would behave according to a standard typographic grid, but in three dimensions, so that multiple axes could work together to organize the text.

Several kinds of information are presented: a selection of news articles separated by subject; a complex set of financial data; a geographical map of the United States; and a virtual map of network users joined over the Internet.

project
Dynamic text interface
Digital presentation
Proprietary software

client
TED Conferences LLC
Technology, Entertainment
and Design Conferences
Los Angeles, CA

design
MIT Media Lab
Visible Language Workshop
Muriel Cooper [CD]
David Small
Cambridge, MA

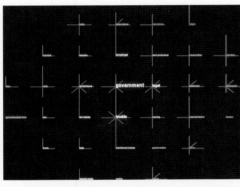
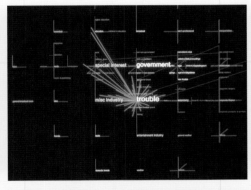
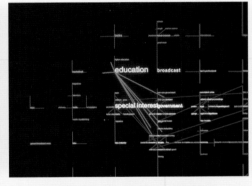

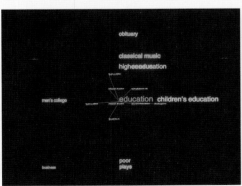
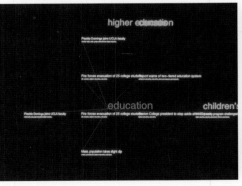

The maps are presented in a kind of space that references location and scale, but the texts are arranged on modular grids that permit the user to fly through the information intuitively, going from one subject to another, turning to an article in space to reveal links to related articles.

The user is able to sort the information contained in the database around the axes of the grid, depending on which path of inquiry he or she wants to follow: each axis shows one set of facts, sorted by specific criteria. The relationships between multiple fact sets are made visible and more immediately accessible through the design's movement; the user can see what information is connected through the grid lines and around corners.

The information's legibility changes depending on its orientation to the viewer. As the user navigates the grid, text that is running along another axis can be rotated into proper reading position; text objects in the distance change color and become more distinct as they come closer.

2

Breaking Grid

Historical Interlude
The Seeds of Deconstruction

Until the late twentieth century, the design industry tended to focus on the more or less steadily increasing influence of rationalism when it traced its development or promoted itself, and with good reason: emphasizing the pragmatic, rational aspects of design helps clients understand and trust the design industry as a resource. But every field of artistic endeavor comprises different schools of thought, some of them contradictory, and graphic design is no exception.

Just as the use of grids in modern design practice grew from developments in technology, aesthetic thought, and industrialization, the use of alternate, intuitive methods of composition—prevalent in current design practice—grew from these same influences. Along with the marvels of mechanized production came a proficiency at cruelty and destruction. The late nineteenth and early twentieth centuries were plagued by war on a scale that was previously unknown, facilitated by such innovations as the Gatling gun, tanks, grenades, and mines. This madness, coupled with Sigmund Freud's publications about the human psyche, fueled an exploration of the absurd and primal in art and design. As early as the 1880s, a tendency toward primal image making as a reaction to the devastation of machines and war began to find a voice: Art Nouveau's sensual plant imagery signaled a pursuit of the individual, organic, and idiosyncratic in design; Expressionism's aggressive works showed a preoccupation with suffering in the human condition; Dada and Surrealism explored the subconscious, dream states, and the absurdities of language.

A New Visual Reality These latter movements began as reactions to World War I. Co-opting the strange, new language of visual abstraction, the Dadaists applied it to verbal language to express their horror over the war.

In 1914, the poet Hugo Ball opened the Cabaret Voltaire in Zurich as a meeting place for poets, writers, musicians, and artists who shared this outrage. They included Tristan Tzara, who prepared their manifestos and edited the magazine *DADA*; Jean Arp, a painter and sculptor; and later Marcel Duchamp, a painter who began his career as a Cubist but was more fascinated by symbolism and linguistic games. Language and experience became bound in Dada's explosive word poems and nonsense posters where words failed to correspond to any explicit meaning. In Dada, letters and words are pictures of emotional or psychological states, and their power comes from aggressive visual arrangements signifying those states, not as carriers of literal meaning. Dada's use of type as image was similar to that of other movements, like Futurism, in which the visual treatment of information was also used as a pictorial vehicle for the viewer's associations. Filippo Marinetti, Futurism's founder, used repeated letterform patterns and dynamic scale and placement to convey ideas about sound, motion, and the violent power of machines.

Cubist and Symbolist poets in France also explored the syntactic portrayal of writing through typography based on its spoken or verbal attributes. Stéphane Mallarmé and Guillaume Appolinaire created word pictures in poems and essays in which page structure was defined by the image. Appolinaire's now-famous concrete poem "Il Pleut" ("It's Raining") is organized in vertical lines that resemble a picture of rain. Appolinaire and poets like him were influenced by semiotics, the study of signs, from the writings of Charles Pierce, an American, and Ferdinand de Saussure of France.

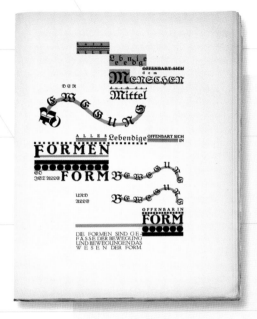

This poeticizing of visual expression—characterized by visual word play and the signification of subject matter or actual experience by unrelated signs—was becoming a trend in graphic design that would run counter to the steady development of rationalism.

Order and Disorder United Collage was another new visual analogy that built on the reenvisioning of form begun in Cubism, which juxtaposed found images in dynamic relationships where chance could play a role in the perception of meaning. The Berlin Dadaists Hanna Hoch and Raoul Hausemann were among the first known artists to employ collage. The designer and artist Kurt Schwitters, who worked in Hanover, is particularly notable for helping to establish both grid-based and irrational systems in design. Schwitters's work as a Dadaist was supported by his business as an advertising designer with prestigious accounts. His output of collaged typographic clippings and refuse alternated with professional posters and layouts for magazines, including his own, *Merz,* which featured articles and visual essays based on his nonsense poems. Schwitters collaborated with Theo van Doesburg and El Lissitsky on several occasions, blending his Constructivist interests with those of Dada.

Schwitters is one of several designers in the twentieth century who helped assimilate and institutionalize nonrational design approaches, particularly typography, alongside those being pursued by rational structuralists.

The close association of irrational and rational approaches was also evident in the Weimar Bauhaus before the school made a decisive shift toward rationalism in its curriculum. Johannes Itten, a member of the *Blaue Reiter* group of painters that also included Wassily Kandinsky, was instrumental in setting up the Bauhaus foundation curriculum which, among other things, stressed the exploration of personally derived abstract mark making. Itten's experiments in the type shop, before Moholy-Nagy replaced him in 1923, had begun to incorporate painterly, nonrectilinear composition and the use of elements from the type case: he used lines of lead, usually reserved for spacing, as a decorative element to visually enhance the emphasis within type. In his 1921 publication, *Utopia*, Itten's compositions merge concrete symbolist poetry and idiosyncratic expression with intuitively structured pages.

During the same period in the Netherlands, designers like Piet Zwart were approaching the new abstraction from a different perspective. Dutch design already had a history of innovation and intriguing use of symbolic, abstract form dating back to Symbolist and Jugendstil designers like Jan Toorop and Johan Thorn-Prikker in the late 1800s. Zwart's use of montage and typographic expressionism blended this Symbolist approach, the de Stijl purity of primary color, and the dynamic composition of Dada and Futurism. Zwart's work for clients like NKF, an industrial cable manufacturing company, walked a line between the structural and the intuitive, appropriately drawing on both systems of thinking as dictated by the catalogue's content.

Zürcher Maler
Zurich Painters
Poster
Emil Ruder
From *Typography*, published
by Niggli Verlag, Zurich, 1960

Dada
Typographic study
*After similar
studies designed by
Emil Ruder*

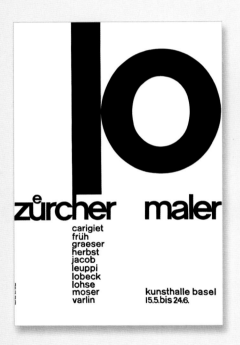

World War II scattered and isolated a number of designers. In Switzerland, the painterly, symbolic approach of Ernst Keller had merged with the mathematical and architectural precision of Zurich grid advocates like Josef Müller-Brockmann and Carlo Vivarelli. Keller's former student, Armin Hoffmann, pursued elemental visual composition in his work and as director of the Basel design school, where he enlisted Emil Ruder as typography teacher. Both Ruder's work and teaching method focused on typography that derived from a structural perspective, but he also focused on clearly integrating it with imagery by stressing its pictorial potential. Unlike Müller-Brockmann, Ruder freely mixed weight, slant, and size changes, even within single lines of type, to achieve a semiotic representation of language. In his 1960 book, *Typography,* Ruder devotes several pages to a discussion of grids, but nowhere near as much space as he devotes to the exposition of type as an image with intrinsic visual qualities that cannot be ignored. The paradox of Ruder's work is that his rigorous approach to examining type's visual, semantic qualities led him not only to anticipate the appearance of deconstructive work among his students, but to create it himself. In his experiments using the Univers family of typefaces, for example, he visually communicates notions about physical or emotional state in compositions like *Jazz,* splitting up and crossing columns diagonally by aligning words on an angle. Other experiments in which he expresses the meaning of words by altering their visual construction or breaking them apart show that he was investigating ideas initiated by Dada and Futurist designers in the 1920s, like Marinetti and Schwitters. Seen this way, Ruder's work can be described as a nexus point in codifying those syntactic and semiotic experiments within the framework of the International Style as it was developing; that is, he actively helped assimilate the seeds of grid deconstruction into the rational aesthetic of structuralist graphic design. As a teacher, his experiments and interaction with his students would become profoundly influential.

Against the Establishment By the mid-1960s, the International Style was becoming entrenched as a design methodology in Europe and the United States. Students from the Basel and Zurich schools—and also from the Kunstgewerbeschule in Ulm, Germany (founded, in part, by Max Bill)—were disseminating its reductive, minimal aesthetic. Corporations benefited from the unifying and cost-efficient aspects of the grid-based identity systems that these students advocated. But as the younger design community—along with everyone else—continued its recovery from the second World War, it was becoming increasingly critical of established ways of thinking, increasingly wary of corporate and governmental motives, and increasingly interested in opposing the kind of classist impulses that had repressed and brutalized specific groups of people in the war. In the United States, the civil rights movement drew attention to disenfranchised groups; revolutions in Cuba and China evinced similar kinds of unrest. In the midst of the International Style's methodical efficiency, a search for expression based on personal experience and narrative was catalyzed by the visceral thump of rock n' roll, the sexual revolution, and the rise of popular youth culture. Pyschedelia, television, and a rediscovery of Art Nouveau gave rise to design idioms and countermovements that don't fit neatly into

Austellung
Poster
Wolfgang Weingart
Courtesy of
Wolfgang Weingart

Was ich morgen...
Typographic study
Wolfgang Weingart
Courtesy of
Wolfgang Weingart

the bigger trends: Victor Moscoso and Haight-Ashbury psychedelic rock posters on the West Coast of America; Milton Glaser, Seymour Chwast, and the idiosyncratic, historical illustrative style of the PushPin Group; and the "big idea" conceptual advertising of Bob Gill, Bill Bernbach, and Henry Wolf. These and other approaches flourished in the 1960s and 1970s despite the International Style; they worked around Modernism, reflecting impulses from outside and quietly influencing dramatic changes that would happen within.

In Basel, Emil Ruder's students were engaged in studying fundamental typographic principles when a young typesetter's apprentice from Stuttgart joined the school. Wolfgang Weingart had been trained in a traditional German type shop, but had been exposed to the work of Hofmann, Müller-Brockman, and Ruder by an older apprentice; fascinated by the unfamiliar

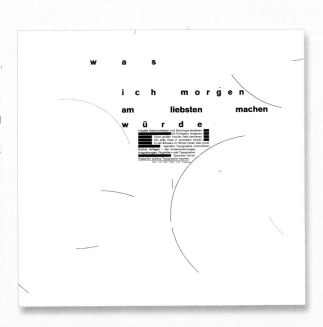

image-oriented typographic approach of the Swiss, he had come to Basel in 1964 to be trained as a designer. His personal experiments in the type shop, where he incorporated the accidental printing of letterpress material—like the lead lines used to separate individual lines of type and the bottom side of lead letters—had given him entry to the school. But Ruder's methodical exploration of typographic nuance intimidated and bored Weingart, who was more comfortable making images with elements from the type case. Having absorbed a good deal of Swiss thinking in his apprenticeship, however, Weingart began his own systematic exploration of typographic form, but with a marked difference: it extrapolated the idea of visually semantic composition—type that bases its visual form on the verbal structure of the words it represents—beyond the functional presentation sought by Ruder, and into a personal, idiosyncratic and texturally expressive approach akin to painting. Weingart looked at the understructures and absolute formal qualities of the material he was working with as indicators of potential new ways to compose. Highlighting groups of words in

proximity to each other with reversed-out white areas created secondary sentences playing in the paragraph; filling in the negative spaces created by the ragged edge of a paragraph added architectural impact on a page; and combining letterforms into new shapes or spacing them out in self-consciously visual arrangements emphasized their structural qualities or made reference to forms in the environment. In essence, Weingart uncovered a new visual potential for language by decon-

structing it, and the significance of this work was profound. It implied that rational structure—the grid—could be one of many possible systems for organizing visual material, and that context is an important factor in determining which system is best for a specific project.

The Iconoclasts and the Academy   In 1968, Armin Hofmann asked Weingart to teach. At the same time, Weingart was being asked to lecture and show his work around the world. His typographical approach, in concert with the teaching of Hofmann, influenced generations of Basel students. The individuality of his approach was especially appealing to young design students, who were now coming to Basel from a number of countries. Among them were Americans like April Greiman, a student of Basel graduates Hans U. Allemann, Inge Druckrey, and Christine Zelinsky at the Kansas City Art Institute in Missouri. Weingart's dimensional approach to space and his mixing of textures had a tremendous impact on her design process. After she returned to America, Greiman freelanced and taught in Philadelphia, Boston, and New York, eventually landing in Los Angeles in the early 1980s.

Greiman began experimenting with various emerging technologies, like video, in combination with found images and conventional printing techniques, which continued to define the new visual language of Basel and similarly-oriented design schools. Organization and treatment of visual material was being driven by intuition and direct, visceral response to its optical and conceptual qualities. Other students, as well as those who went on to teach—at schools like Philadelphia College of Art and Carnegie Mellon—and to work in New York and Los Angeles, brought the mixture of discipline and experimentation with them. A "New Wave" of Swiss and Swiss-trained designers—Dan Friedman, Valerie Pettis, Willi Kunz, Steff Geissbuhler, Chris Myers—joined Greiman and others in assimilating this new development into the mainstream of design practice.

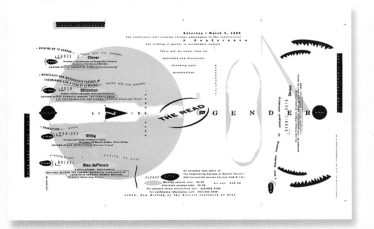

New Discourses in Form   In 1970, a recently graduated industrial designer in Chicago named Katherine McCoy found herself in a graphic design position at Unimark International, working in the minimal Swiss International Style that Unimark was employing to reshape the corporate visual world. After a year, she began to teach graphic design at Cranbrook, an art and design academy in Michigan with a long history of involvement in avant-garde architecture. McCoy's initial curricula were derivative of the grid-based typographic methods she had become accustomed to at Unimark. But in the experimental and highly intellectual environment of Cranbrook, she and her fellow faculty began to consider the visual system they were perpetuating. By this time, Weingart's experiments were becoming widely known; in addition, the writings of architects Robert Venturi and Denise Scott-Brown were having a wide impact. Their seminal 1972 book, *Learning from Las Vegas*, helped establish a radical new regard for the vernacular: rather than dismiss garish, naïve, and popular visual expressions like drive-ins and gambling strips, designers could incorporate these idiosyncratic forms as a way of resonating on a more personal level with their audiences. McCoy's close friend (and later Cranbrook student), Edward Fella, was particularly interested in vernacular signage and lettering; others began to explore game show iconography, historic type forms, and coding systems as

sources for image and type interaction that would create a graphic counterpart to the ideas Venturi and Scott-Brown were propagating.

Political and social concerns came to the forefront of designers' minds once again; at Cranbrook and on the West Coast, these pop culture deformations were giving voice to dicussions about race, gender, and class by visually distinguishing them from the smooth veneer of the corporate International Style. A second result was that they also separated from what they considered an East Coast/European design establishment. Many designers from that establishment viewed the work at Cranbrook through a filter that categorized it as either simply ugly or as morally wrong, a repudiation of the progress for which Modernism had struggled. Within the design counterculture, however, the sense that they were exploring a late form of Modernism, a self-critical and mannered form, pervaded their experiments. During the period between 1971 and 1984, the word *deconstruction* was coined as a description of what these experiments were trying to accomplish: to break apart preconceived structures or to use those structures as a starting point to find new ways of making verbal and visual connections between images and language. In addition to Venturi and Scott-Brown's writings, poststructuralist philosophy and semiotics were filtering into the mix. McCoy's work, for example, started with grid-based structures and began to shift elements out of the primary structure, as in her recruiting posters; other approaches involved introducing extra space between words or lines of type within running text to focus attention on

the grammar. Looking at these distinctions and then rebuilding exaggerated configurations of type and image based on the findings became the hallmark of work produced at Cranbrook by designers like Robert Nakata, Allen Hori, Lorraine Wilde, Lucille Tenazas, Scott Santoro, Laurie Haycock, and P. Scott Makela. This work showed evidence of literary influences like that of the poststructural philosopher Michel Foucault and the semiotician Roland Barthes, as well as visual influences from the Swiss New Wave. In most cases, it eschewed conventional notions of beauty in favor of tense, unfamiliar combinations of texture and language.

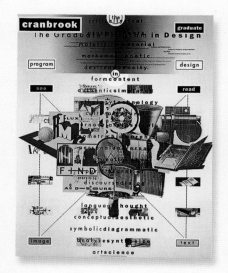

Sci-Arc Summer Programs
Poster
April Greiman
Courtesy of April Greiman

Contemporary Improvised Music
Poster
Allen Hori/Studio Dumbar
Courtesy of Allen Hori

Tulipstoolong
Poster
Allen Hori
Courtesy of Allen Hori

Hanging at Carmine Street: Beach Culture
Periodical page spread
David Carson
Courtesy of David Carson

The Second Industrial Revolution While the mainstream design community struggled to understand the intellectualized conversation going on at Cranbrook, the computer happened. Apple Computer's 1984 introduction of the desktop computer with a graphical interface yielded a revolution in design practice similar in scale to that of the Industrial Revolution of the 1780s. Designers were quick to assimilate the new technology for the rapid and seamless manipulation of image and type that its programs facilitated.

April Greiman's work incorporated the image-editing capability of the computer into her process of hybridizing media, typography, and perceptual space. The design developments at Cranbrook were catalyzed by these same new capabilities; texture, image, and type could now be manipulated in exotic combinations that extrapolated their already challenging deconstructions into three-dimensional space.

The Dutch design community, having historically provided a proving-ground for visual innovations in the commercial world, not only embraced these technological and theoretical developments, but hosted a continuing series of interns and expatriate graduates from American design schools. Allen Hori and Robert Nakata, both graduates of Cranbrook, for example, found themselves working at Studio Dumbar, already distinguished for its conceptual use of photography and surreal spatial typography for large Dutch corporations.

From an Unexpected Quarter The shift from traditional hand skills to digital designing and production introduced high-level digital editing and typesetting to a vast audience; in this way, the assimilation of vernacular modes of expression was complemented by a reverse assimilation of design craft by individuals who weren't trained as graphic designers.

David Carson epitomized this shift. A surfer and sociology graduate, Carson came to design by working at *Beach Culture*, a California surf magazine. His unstudied layouts relied on an intuitive sense of placement that spoke more about interpreting the experience of the content, not about rationally or impartially organizing it.

By using the extensive typesetting capabilities of the computer, Carson was able to explore typographic arrangements and effects that had been impossible before its invention: overlapping lines of type and letters that flipped backwards and forwards, dense textures of type and image, and columns of type whose contours weren't parallel—or, for that matter, straight lines at all. Where the Cranbrook experiments were still

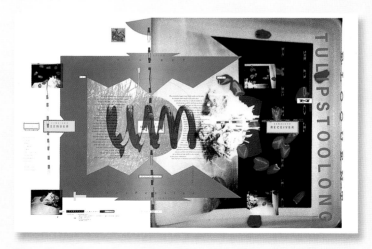

Raygun
Periodical spreads
David Carson
Courtesy of David Carson

Typography Now
Book pages
WhyNot Associates
Published by Booth-Clibborn Editions, 1991
Courtesy of Andy Bell

Eight Days in Venice
Broadsides
WhyNot Associates
Student work produced at
Royal College of Art, 1987

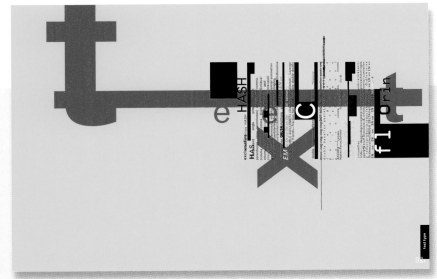

This type of system for generating visual cohesion through intuitive, spontaneous relationships was further popularized by the work of the American type publishers Emigre, by British designers like Siobahn Keaney and Jonathan Barnbrook, and by firms like Why Not Associates. In project after project, these designers were violating conventional ideas about structure in favor of organization that reflected ideas about time, film, and the expanding world of digital interactivity.

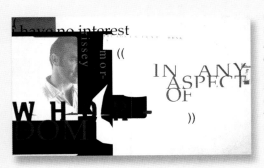

referring to the idea of structure, Carson's work ignored it. In his design of the culture magazine *Raygun,* published between 1991 and 1996, no overarching structure exists, yet every issue is recognizably related; the ferocity of the layouts and the continual destruction of conformity on every page visually define a system that is identifiable and understandable, despite the lack of a consistent editorial grid structure.

As designers have assimilated the computer's visual capabilities and its ubiquitous presence in daily life—as well as innovations from Weingart, Cranbrook, and Carson—the notion of experientially driven presentation has gained importance as a viable, user-centric method for organizing information. Interactive media, in particular, has helped change the way people access and process the information with which they're presented. Intuitive and idiosyncratic approaches to organization participate on equal terms with rational approaches based on grid structures. The designer's set of tools now includes several methods for conveying ideas from which the designer can choose the most appropriate for a given project.

Exploring Other Options
A Guide to Grid Deconstruction and
Nonstructural Design Approaches

Grid structure in typography and design has become part of
the status quo of designing, but as recent history has shown,
there are numerous other ways to organize information and
images. The decision whether to use a grid always comes
down to the nature of the content in a given project.

Sometimes that content has its own internal structure that
a grid won't necessarily clarify; sometimes the content
needs to ignore structure altogether to create specific kinds
of emotional reactions in the intended audience; sometimes
a designer simply envisions a more complex intellectual
involvement on the part of the audience as part of their
experience of the piece.

The public's ability to apprehend and digest information has become more sophisticated over time as well; constant bombardment of information from sources like television, film, and interactive digital media have created a certain kind of expectation for information to behave in particular ways. One has only to look at television news broadcasting or reality-based programming, where several kinds of presentation—oral delivery, video, still images and icons, and moving typography—overlap or succeed each other in rapid edits, to understand that people have become accustomed to more complex, designed experiences. In an effort to create a meaningful impression that competes with, and distinguishes itself within, this visual environment, designers have pursued various new ways of organizing visual experience.

The vigorous composition of this typographic poster defies the rational approach of grid-based design.

A loose structure is implied by the horizontal linear divisions created by secondary type like the date, but otherwise the layout is entirely intuitive.

Its strength, however, lies in this dynamic, instinctive positioning and treatment of forms. The raw texture of the letters and background, the overlapping of forms that refer to the legible information create a kinetic experience that is both filmic and reminiscent of tattered street posters.

FONDAZIONE BEVILACQUA LA MASA COMUNE DI VENEZIA

CARSON/venezia

a ARv

ON

15 settembre–4 ottobre 1996
orario 9.00/19.00 chiuso il martedì

galleria della fondazione

Bevilacqua La Masa

MASA

Grid Deformations
Structural sketches
Kristie Williams

Dualities of the Grid
Broadsides
Jenny Chan

 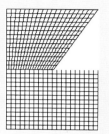 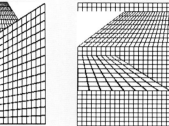 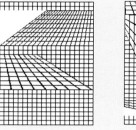 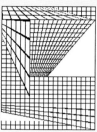

A simple modular grid, without gutters between modules, is the starting point for a dimensional deconstruction. Groups of flowlines and column lines are distorted to explore possibilities of exaggerated illusory space and dimensionality.

The results of this kind of "structural deconstruction" can be seen in this set of broadsides that investigates the nature of the grid. A classical two-column Roman manuscript structure sequentially gives way to a three-dimensional space where columns intersect, overlap, and rotate into each other.

Grid Deconstruction

As the word itself implies, the purpose of *deconstructing* is to deform a rationally structured space so that the elements within that space are forced into new relationships: or, simply put, beginning with a grid and altering it to see what happens. That said, it's probably clear that there's no real set of rules that can be applied to the process of deconstructing. But if the goal is to find new spatial or visual relationships by breaking down a structure, it's helpful to at least begin thinking about that process in a methodical way. The first idea that might come to mind as a way of looking at this process is to think about splitting apart a conventional grid—even a very simple one.

A structure can be altered in any number of ways. First, a designer might experiment with "cutting" apart major zones and shifting them—horizontally or vertically. It's important to watch what happens when information that would normally appear in an expected place—marking a structural juncture in the grid—is moved to another place, perhaps aligned with some other kind of information in a way that creates a new verbal connection that didn't exist before. The shifted information may wind up behind or on top of some other information if a change in size or density accompanies the shift in placement. The optical confusion this causes might be perceived as a surreal kind of space where foreground and background swap places.

Shifting or breaking apart grid modules or columns so that they begin to overlap, even while they carry sequential information (like running text), can create a perception of layers within the compositional space. The textures of different columns interacting as they run over each other can create a sense of transparency where the viewer perceives the columns of text, or other

elements, to be floating in front of each other. A conventional grid structure repeated in different orientations could be used to explore a more dynamic architectural space by creating different axes of alignment. For example, two- and three-column grids, in different scales and at opposing angles to each other, will create new spatial zones that interlock. Similarly, overlapping grids with modules of different proportions, or which run at different angles in relation to each other, can introduce a kind of order to the spatial and directional ambiguity that layering creates, especially if some elements are oriented on both layers simultaneously. This kind of architectonic deconstruction emphasizes the visual qualities of multiple structures interacting; changes in scale or density within these structures can help to distinguish specific types of information as well as create an interactive, yet still geometric and understandable, space.

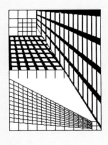
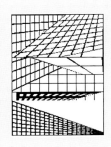
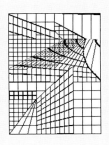

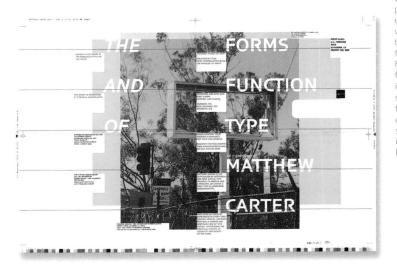

Although the base grid that underpins this small poster's composition is evident, its rigor has been violated in subtle ways that aren't so obvious at first: the title type baseline has slipped under the red flowlines; the background image consists of two shifting planes of tonality that throw space into question. In addition, a simple verbal breakdown in the title hints at another kind of deconstruction....

Taking Things Apart...
Poster
Steff Geissbühler

French Currents of the Letter
Journal pages
Katherine McCoy

Frameworkin' It
Typographic study
Young Kim

Both informational and conceptual, the verbal deconstruction of the title derives from chemical names in this exhibition poster designed for a pharmaceutical company. The deconstruction visually treats the title type, as well as communicates the nature of the company's particular business.

Linguistic deconstruction is used here to visually represent the vocal "journey" through the poem. Cadence, phrasing, and concrete vocal emphasis are indicated through intuitive changes in scale and treatment.

Liguistic Deconstruction

Verbal or conceptual cues within the content can also be used to break a grid structure. The natural rhythm of spoken language, for example, is often used as a guide for changing weight, size, color, or alignment among lines type; louder or "faster" words may be set in larger or bolder type or in italics, corresponding to stresses and lulls in actual speech. Giving a "voice" to visual language can help alter the structure of a text by pushing words out of paragraphs or forcing modules or columns into relationships where the natural logic of the writing creates a visual order. For example, treating all of the adjectives in a particular way would create a secondary structure with a rhythmic, organic quality. Breaking phrases and words apart in a running text calls attention to the individual parts of speech. As the space between them increases, the text takes on a matrix like appearance and the presumed reading order may begin to change for the reader. Although generally this would interfere with reading, in some cases the resulting ambiguity may be appropriate to the content of the text, yielding associations between words or images that can be used to augment the literal meaning of the text.

In this example, a conventional text is gradually deconstructed over many pages. The designer's process of breaking apart the page form begins with the introduction of space between phrases and then between words; the verbal structure of the essay is brought into focus, while the visual clarity is decreased. The running text becomes a texture where the regularized spaces between words imply multiple reading directions.

Blazer
Promotional posters
Steff Geissbühler

Carson: Die Neue
Sammlung
Poster
David Carson

Chinese Painting
Book pages
SooYoon Kim

In all of these compositions, the designers have relied on their senses of placement, scale, movement, and color to intuitively orchestrate visual qualities within the respective formats.

Spontaneous Optical Composition

Far from being random, this compositional method can be described as purposeful intuitive placement of material based on its formal aspects: seeing the inherent visual relationships and contrasts within the material and making connections for the viewer based on those relationships. Sometimes designers will use this method as a step in the process of building a grid, but its use as an organizational idea on its own is just as valid.

This approach starts fast and loose: the designer works with the material much like a painter does, making quick decisions as the material is put together and the relationships are first seen. As the different optical qualities of the elements begin to interact, the designer can determine which qualities are affected by those initial decisions and make adjustments to enhance or negate the qualities in whatever way is most appropriate for the communication.

The method's inherent liveliness has an affinity with collage; its sense of immediacy and directness can be very inviting to viewers, providing them with a simple and gratifying experience that is very accessible. The result is a structure that is dependent on the optical tensions of the composition and their connection to the information hierarchy within the space.

Drowning
Typographic explorations
Le Van Ho

Kansas
Study of vernacular image
Jessica Berardi

A personal narrative about a near-death incident begins with a straight-forward column structure that is deconstructed in successive studies to evoke the motion of floodwaters and the desperate nature of the situation.

Conceptual or Pictorial Allusion

Another interesting way of creating compositions is to derive a visual idea from the content and impose it on the page format as a kind of arbitrary structure. The structure can be an illusory representation of a subject, like waves or the surface of water, or may be based on a concept, like a childhood memory, a historical event, or a diagram. Whatever the source of the structural idea, the designer can then use it to organize material in such a way that it refers to the idea. For example, text and images might sink underwater or float around like objects caught in a flood. Even though no grid is present, sequential compositions are given a kind of unity because of the governing idea. Margins, intervals between images and text, and relative depth on the page may constantly change, but this change has recognizable features that relate to the overall idea; these might even be called allusive structures.

In projects of a sequential nature, like books or walls in an exhibit, visual elements relate to each other in time, as though in frames of a film. Images might move across a format or be otherwise changed from page to page, affecting other images or text that appear later. This kind of kinetic structure is amorphous—it literally has no distinguishable shape—except that its effects can be recognized and understood as the viewer experiences the succession of frames. A simple example of this visual kinesis as a structure might be a sequence of pages where text appears to advance forward in space because its scale changes incrementally every time the page is turned. Using sensory experiences of space and time as organizing principles can be a powerful tool for evoking a visceral, emotional response from viewers.

Images and typography communicate a specific cultural history in this poster study. Vernacular type styles and relevant images are arranged in ways that suggest other images: a flag and a landscape are most apparent.

A master grid orchestrates
the disection of an image
across multiple pages of a
book. The decisions about
where the disection takes
place are made arbitrarily,
without regard to the composition within the image
itself. Furthermore, a for-
mula for where to place
the dissected pieces in the
page sequence is predetermined but, again, without
knowing what the results
will be in advance.

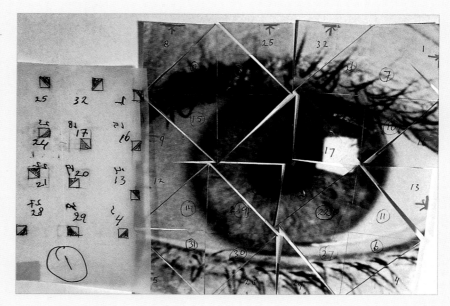

Chance Operation

The use of chance as an organizing principal
might seem counterintuitive. The unpredictable
results, however, can often aid in communication
from a conceptual standpoint by bringing out
juxtapositions of material that might otherwise
have escaped notice.

Conducting a chance operation implies that the
chance is being controlled to a certain degree,
and this is usually the case: a designer might
fling paint at a surface, knowing that certain
kinds of patterns will occur because of the size
of the brush or the specific gesture; increasing
the point size of selected type in a composition
without adjusting its starting position may
result in an unusually organic composition. In
a similar operation, cropped images might be
physically scattered or dropped from a certain
height over a format. The resulting random
placement could be useful in communicating
ideas about motion, the unpredictability of
nature, absurdity, and so on. By selecting the
type of chance operation to use, a designer can
skew the results in their favor to some degree,
ensuring appropriateness in the form while

allowing the unpredictability to create new visual
relationships that structured thinking about layout
won't achieve. A designer might even use a grid to
give direction to specific kinds of chance, knowing
that the underlying structure will cause the
chance results to behave in (hopefully) desirable
ways that illuminate the content while creating
the same kind of unexpected visual compositions
at the end of the process. For example, a designer
might arbitrarily apply a matrix to a large image
to determine how to crop it for different pages,
but the shape of the cropping and the resulting
details might provide interesting texture or connect conceptually with a text. Sometimes, introducing chance into the design process helps a
designer see the material more clearly, allowing
him or her to organize it in less predictable, yet
more illuminating, ways.

Key to Exhibit Notation

The diagram below shows a typical page spread for the Exhibit sections. The notations provided for each exhibit feature selected information for quick reference and a simple system for comparing related works in both sections (see also *Making the Grid, Exhibits*, page 32), grid-based or not.

These comparisons are meant as a catalyst for analysis. Sometimes the relationship between exhibits being compared is plainly structural, at other times it's less explicit; in some cases, the comparison is between exhibits that show opposing qualities.

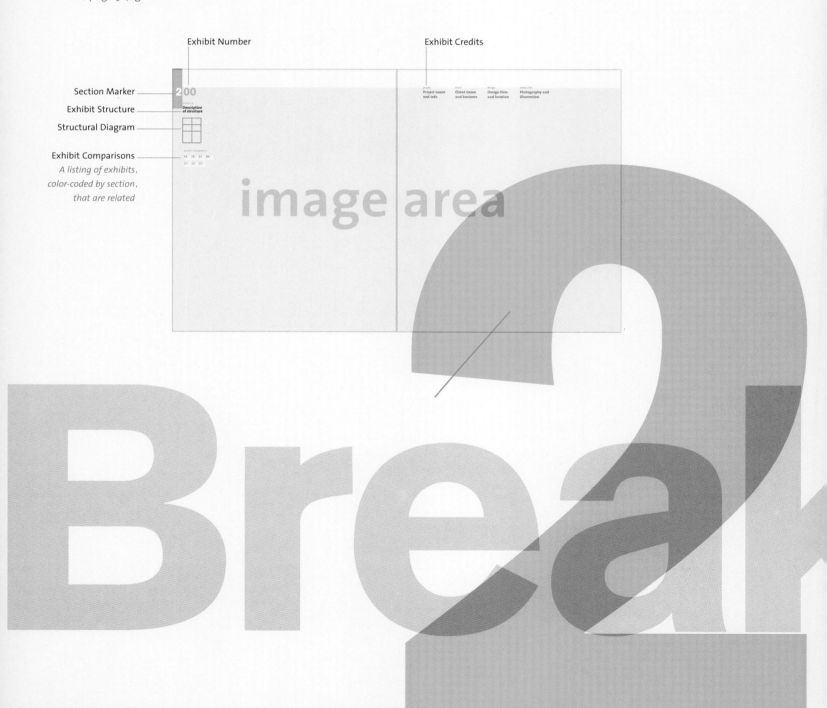

Exhibit Number

Exhibit Credits

Section Marker

Exhibit Structure

Structural Diagram

Exhibit Comparisons
A listing of exhibits, color-coded by section, that are related

image area

Break

Exhibits
Grid Deconstructions and Non-Grid-Based Design Projects

structure

Manuscript grid deconstruction

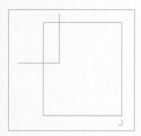

exhibit comparisons

project
**Radical Graphics/
Graphic Radicals**
Book
*Case bound with
translucent printed wrapper
Offset lithography*

client
Chronicle Books
Publisher
San Francisco, CA

design
McCoy & McCoy
Katherine McCoy
Buena Vista, CO

The deconstruction of a manuscript grid gives a quiet yet wry context for a book exhibiting the work of radical graphic designers. Ample margins, larger outside than at top, set the text block low on the page. The blocks mirror each other across the gutter. The proportions seem at first to be the only unconventional aspect of the classical structure; however, structural details in the typography reveal there's more to it. Images intrude into the main text block as needed, carving out large blocks of the column. This same deleting of a portion of the column provides space for captions accompanying the exhibited work. In some instances the captions practically butt the alignment of the primary text block, creating tension and an uncertainty in space.

Irregular negative shapes—elipses and diagonals—independent of image, cut into the primary text block, sometimes reinforced by similarly shaped captions. Conflicting alignment relationships, in which a justified column is greeted by a caption set flush-right (or more jarring, a caption which is also justified and shifted off baseline by a few points) add subversive detailing to the compositions.

structure

Modular grid deconstruction via chance operation

exhibit comparisons

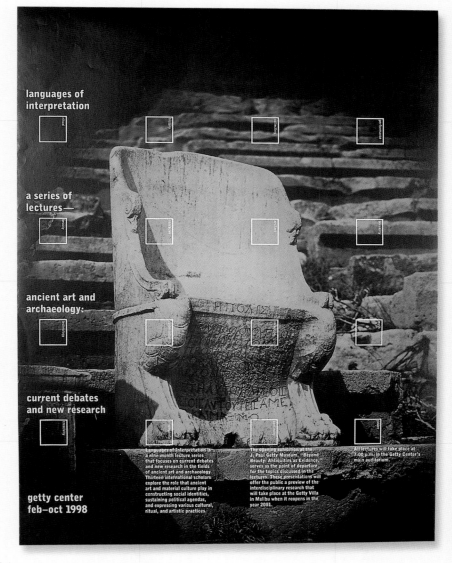

A physical breaking of the grid used to organize material in this poster creates the layout of the resulting brochure. When the poster is cut down, images and information from the two sides are juxtaposed in a new structure. The resulting brochure—full-bleed texture and symbolic title on the left, informational caption enclosed in a corresponding square on the right—retains a recognizably modular structure, but the background images are left to bleed unexpectedly out of the new format.

The most interesting aspect of this project is its literal exposition of the conceptual. The content, a series of lectures organized around the theme "Languages of Interpretation," is made explicit not only through the interpretation of the material as both a poster and as a booklet (each a distinct structural language), but also through the potential for interpreting the juxtapositions between symbolic key words, lecture titles, and images.

project
**Languages of
Interpretation**
Poster/brochure
Offset lithography

client
Getty Research Institute
Art and art historical
research and museums
Los Angeles, CA

design
Praxis
Simon Johnston
Los Angeles, CA

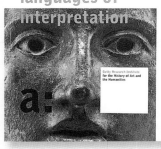

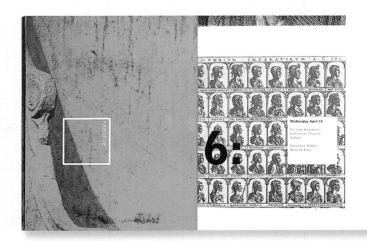

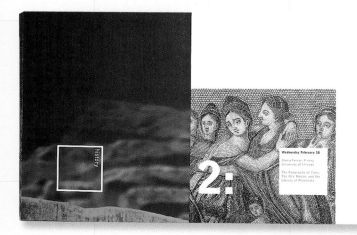

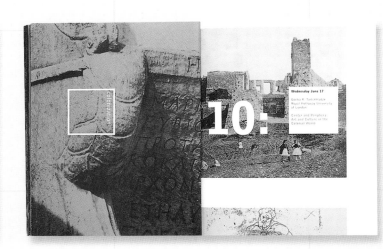

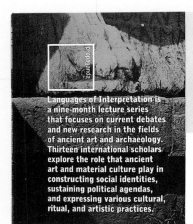

project
Niklaus Troxler, Posters
1977-1999
Exhibition Poster
Silkscreened in black

client
Willisau Rathaus
Exhibition space
Willisau, Switzerland

design
Niklaus Troxler Design
Niklaus Troxler
Willisau, Switzerland

structure
**Verbal/conceptual
deconstructions**

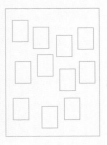

project
ImproPlakate
Improvised Posters
Exhibition poster
Silkscreen, two colors

client
Willisau Rathaus
Exhibition space
Willisau, Switzerland

design
Niklaus Troxler Design
Niklaus Troxler
Willisau, Switzerland

Each of these posters uses a verbal, or semiotic, cue relating to the poster format as a means of deconstructing the informational language within.

The poster at left deconstructs the format with itself. The stark, dramatic layout of black type in a white field shows the conceptual repetition inherent in the project—a poster about a show of posters.

The designer organizes the informational type along the upper left and top edge of a blank format, similar to the format of the poster itself. Repeating this structure as-is on top of itself and moving downward, a sense of many layers of posters is created, along with a striking organic interplay of black-and-white linear type elements. Repeating the poster format on top of itself, eventually bleeding outward beyond the poster's real format, elevates the communication to a sophisticated level where the image becomes signifier and signified, a poster that shows a posting of posters.

In the deceptively simple poster for an exhibition of posters on the theme "improvisation," the designer uses two spatial levels—one for the exhibit title, in red, one for the event information, in black—as a way to add additional control to a carefully randomized layout of letterforms.

No baselines, alignments, or margins here: the letters float freely as though scattered across the poster's format. Careful consideration has been given to the precise placement of the forms, however, so that although their rhythm is made more random in feeling, their legibility isn't impaired—despite the overlap of red and black letterforms that are close in optical color.

structure

Column grid deconstructed by collage

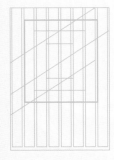

exhibit comparisons

project
AIGA New York
Seasonal events poster
Offset lithography

client
**American Institute of
Graphic Design,
New York Chapter**
Professional designers'
association
New York, NY

design
**Chermayeff & Geismar
Associates**
Steff Geissbuhler
New York, NY

illustration
Steff Geissbuhler
New York, NY

A modularly proportioned column grid confronts
an optically arranged composition of elements
relating to the New York City design scene in
this events poster. The textures of paint, film,
clouds, and printing process dot screens play
against each other, against flat areas of color,
and against illusionary three-dimensional
objects. Their interaction is also modulated by
their movement over and through the group of
invisible concentric frames that create a series
of three-dimensional formats within the poster.
The column grid is defined at the bottom edge
of the poster by the paragraphs describing
events and programs; these columns' module
measures define the invisible frames in the primary image portion above. In combination, the
two methods of organizing material enhance
and emphasize the other.

Column grid deconstructed into layers

exhibit comparisons

project
Powerhouse: UK
Exhibition catalogue
Perfect-bound book
Offset lithography

client
**Department of
Trade & Industry**
Government agency
London, England

design
Why Not Associates
London, England

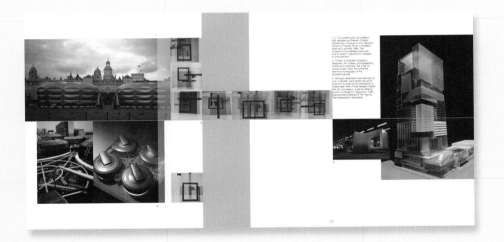

This catalog for an exhibition of British art, fashion, architecture, and industrial design uses overlapping columns as its base structure for text and image arrangement, creating a curtain of shifting planes that moves forward and back depending on the color and density of the texts and images. Images of the exhibits are allowed to expand or contract between the column alignments that occur in each given spread.

Vertical rules are used to increase the tension of particular text alignments, bringing them forward and distinguishing them from others that recede in space. Using this method, unrelated texts are able to run concurrently or even butt up against each other without confusing the reader.

Transparency and shadow resulting from overlaid tints and changes in the density of the typography increase the sense of depth and movement. No two intervals between alignments are the same, so the page structure is one of continuous movement, a metaphor for the British design scene's constant innovation.

structure

Modular grid deconstructed via chance operation

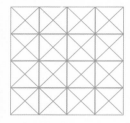

exhibit comparisons

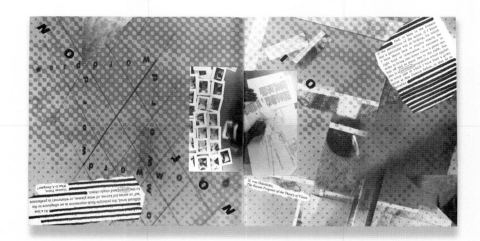

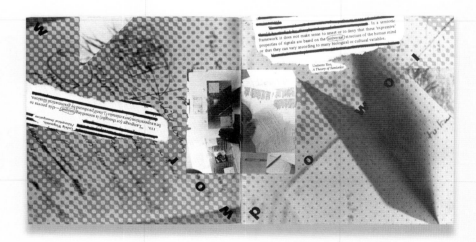

This book of seemingly random three-dimensional spaces, texts, and images is built on a master grid that helps contribute to its intuitive organic quality. This project was completed for an exhibit entitled "Universal/Unique." The exhibit's focus was on the relationship between structure and freedom in design, and participating exhibitors were asked to submit work using predetermined kernel elements: a grid, the word "word," and the image of an eye. The designer set up a modular grid within a square format using the horizontal, vertical, and isometric (45°) axes, and then systematized how each of the kernel elements, plus excerpts from essays and photographs of the

actual design process, would interact with the grid. The square formats together form the layout of a book on a press sheet, and cutting the sheet into book signatures enforces, and yet also denies, properties of the grid. The master "eye" grid, for example, shows its triangular dissection, based on the master grid, which destroys its recognizability but directs the segments' placement from page to page. The excerpted texts, which on one side of the sheet all refer to the idea of universality, come into juxtaposition with the opposing concept, uniqueness, when the pages are cut and folded together.

The grid forces the deconstruction because its structure is created before assessing the material it governs: the material ends up doing whatever it will as it is made to conform to its predetermined criteria. The result is a collage of texture, shadow, light, and type that, upon closer inspection, reveals its hidden order.

project
Chance/Choice
Book, exhibition work
Saddle-stitched booklet
Offset lithography, one color

client
University of the Arts
Graphic Design Department
Educational institution
Philadelphia, PA

design
Thomas Ockerse
Providence, RI

photography
Thomas Ockerse
Providence, RI

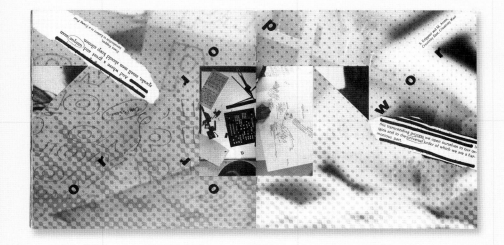

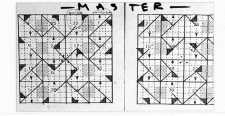

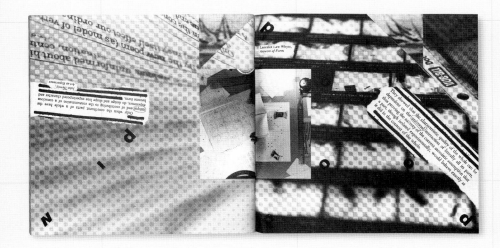

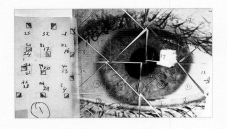

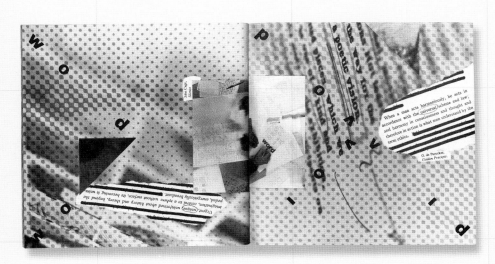

structure

Temporal/filmic column grid deconstruction

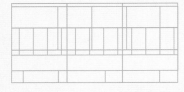

exhibit comparisons

01	05	09	10
13	15	16	23
24	28	30	36
02	05	08	11
14	18	25	26
28	33	37	

This thesis project, "Stopping Time," investigates the relationship between human experience and time by confronting and commenting on them in a series of short films and experimental writings. To stop time is to capture it in some way: to re-capture it, suspend it, sustain it, keep it, hold it, preserve it, or "have" it. My goal is to develop a series of pieces that causes the viewer or reader to think about his or her own relationship to time. The passage of time and our fear of losing the moment drive us in hidden ways. We are unwilling – or perhaps just too busy – to stop and think about it. Our sense of time is a primary means of personal orientation. We attempt to "stop time" by taking snapshots, writing lists, following schedules, and resurrecting the past in order to take hold of the passage of time, to capture it, and to fight loss. The films and the text are a series of individual pieces, parts of which are designed to provide clarity, order, and focus (like the lists we make to time-manage our lives); other parts lead the reader into tangents and associations (like the inevitable onslaught of things which break into our ordered time and lead us astray despite our efforts). From the point of view of content, the pieces will develop ideas about time; from the point of view of experience, they will attempt to put the reader into the whirlwind of time, and the fragmentation of memory.

The visual project is a series of three short films made through a combination of slides and Super 8 film. In the exhibition, the films are seen in a dark, curtained space which viewers walk into. Three separate screens are arranged at different distances away from the viewer so that each film has a different image size. Each film focuses on one notion concerning time and human experience.

When the viewer enters, three separate screens are simultaneously illuminated by the words PAST PRESENT and FUTURE. Each word remains until the film on the corresponding screen begins. This film is sporadically interrupted by the appearance of another film, and by the "Present Ritual" film which is threaded throughout the total course of the piece.

PRESENT

AUDIO: This film is silent.

Time stops sixty times in a minute.

"Then came the film and burst this prison-world asunder by the dynamite of the tenth of a second, so that now, in the midst of its far-flung ruins and debris, we calmly and adventurously go traveling. With the close-up, space expands; with slow motion, movement is extended."
Walter Benjamin, The Work of Art in The Age Of Mechanical Reproduction, p.236

.02   .03   .04   .05

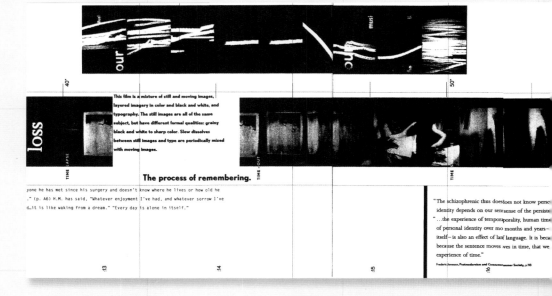

This film is a mixture of still and moving images, layered imagery in color and black and white, and typography. The still images are all of the same subject, but have different formal qualities: grainy black and white to sharp color. Slow dissolves between still images and type are periodically mixed with moving images.

The process of remembering.

...yone he has met since his surgery and doesn't know where he lives or how old he ..." (p. A6) H.M. has said, "Whatever enjoyment I've had, and whatever sorrow I've d...it is like waking from a dream." "Every day is alone in itself."

"The schizophrenic thus does...oes not know personal... identity depends on our sense...sense of the persiste... "...the experience of temporal...porality, human time... of personal identity over mo... months and years... itself – is also an effect of lar... language. It is beca... because the sentence moves... ves in time, that we... experience of time."
Frederic Jameson, Postmodernism and Consumer...consumer Society, p.119

.13   .14   .15   .16

This book documents three related films about the subject of time, which are simultaneously exhibited in a closed environment. Each film is concerned with a different aspect of time: past, present, or future. The book's long, narrow, horizontal format acts as a metaphor for the linear representation of time, much the way a storyboard or score for a film would. Increments in time, as indicated by the frame count of each film displayed in linear sequence on the page, are the organizing principle.

project
Stopping Time:
Past, Present, Future
Film exhibition document

Color laserprint output
bound accordion-fold

school
Yale School of Art
MFA Graphic Design
Educational institution
New Haven, CT

design
Jennifer Bernstein
New York, NY

photography
Jennifer Bernstein
New York, NY

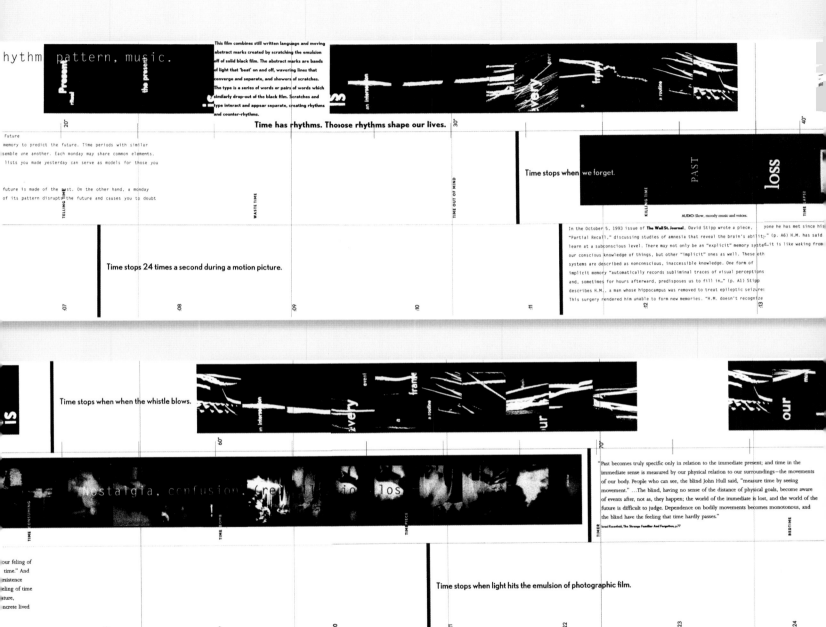

In the exhibition, each film begins and ends in some relation to the other two; in the book, the running text of the essay, as well as the frame sequences of the films, begin in the same relationship: staggered in relationship to each other and staggered in terms of duration and interval. Columns of text follow the frame counts and timing of significant film events that overlap each other and move in synchrony.

The time increments, film events, and frame counts are marked as informational elements, but also form a visual overlay of staggered black rules to give movement and rhythm to the sequence across the panels.

project
Objects in Space
Exhibition poster
Offset lithography

client
American Institute of
Graphics Arts,
Los Angeles chapter
Los Angeles, CA

design
April Greiman
Los Angeles, CA

structure
Spontaneous optical composition

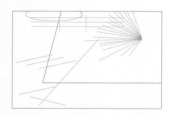

exhibit comparisons

project
**Harry Marks
Achievement Award**
Poster
Offset lithography

client
**Broadcast Designers'
Association International**
Los Angeles, CA

design
April Greiman
Los Angeles, CA

In these two posters, the designer explores the experiential quality of optical space. Neither poster has a recognizable structure, in terms of geometric alignments; further, the hierarchy of information is also in question. The space is organized in a painterly, intuitive way, balancing areas of tension and solidity, like lines of type with open nebulous areas of light and color. Every element acts in concert with the others around it, producing an overall cohesion within the posters as objects or environments, but leaving the viewer free to explore the verbal material as he or she sees fit. The type acts as a constellation within the undefined space that the viewer may interact with at his or her leisure.

structure

Architectonic
column-grid
deconstruction

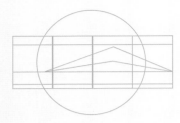

exhibit comparisons

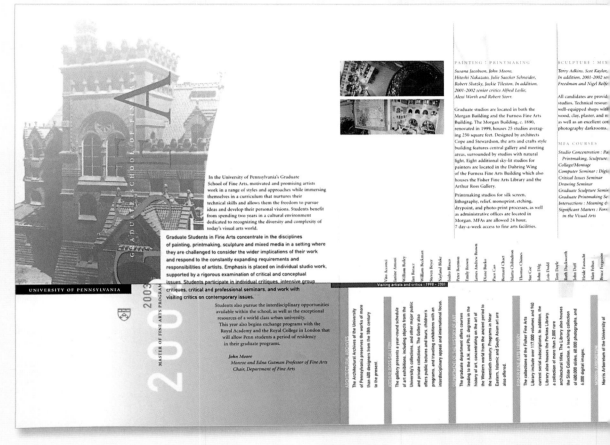

project
Course prospectus
Poster/brochure
Offset lithography
Poster accordion folded to
standard U.S. letter format

client
University of
Pennsylvania Graduate
School of Fine Arts
Educational institution
Philadelphia, PA

design
Paone Design Associates
Gregory Paone
Philadelphia, PA

photography
Jim Abbott
Philadelphia, PA

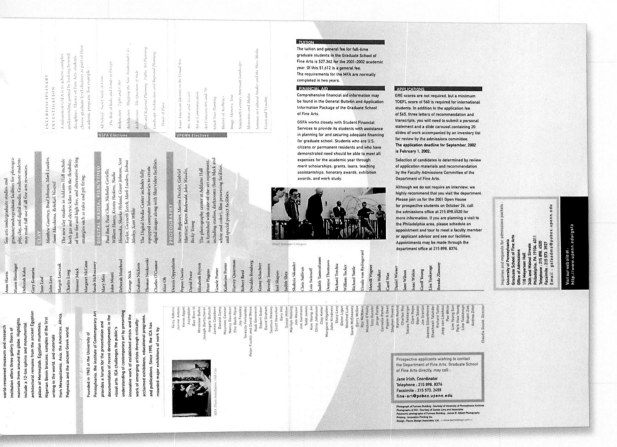

Multiple gridlike structures converge in this foldout course prospectus for a fine-arts educational program. Instances of single columns, triple columns, and modular structures appear, each suited to the nature of the paragraph it is structuring. The long, narrow, horizontal column of visiting artist names, for instance, accommodates what could have been a cumbersome listing in an unexpected way that unifies the four panels and forms a horizon line for the architectural image in the background.

All of the substructures are organized relative to each other, collectively under the influence of the enormous focal circle that links front and back panels and draws the reader into the format from the outside. Each element counteracts and carefully balances the tension or thrust of elements around it. Architectonic vanishing points lock the typography to the implied landscape of buildings where the program is housed.

structure

Column grid
deconstructed by
planar collage

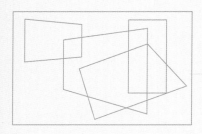

exhibit comparisons

04	05	07	09
13	15	16	23
30	34	36	
02	**05**	**08**	**11**
14	**17**	**33**	**37**

project
Corporate identity
Stationery system and
event invitation
*Offset lithography, four
spot colors*

client
Parsons Dance Company
Professional dance troupe
New York, NY

design
Pettistudio LLC
Valerie Pettis [CD]
Susan Fritz
New York, NY

photography
Lois Greenfield
New York, NY

The identity and print materials for a dance company in New York follow no grid... nor are there any horizontal or strictly vertical elements at all. The system is completely spontaneous, operating off the expression that begins in the logo. Its letters, liberated from the flat, static confines of two-dimensional space, fly against each other like the dancers in the company's performances.

No typography in the system is standardized in terms of placement or size, although the same type family unites all of the materials.

The invitation to an opening night gala incorporates photography of dancers collaged with three-dimensional typography that tilts forward and back in space. The random width of the "columns" of type interact with the figures around them in a rhythmic movement across the panels.

structure
Three-dimensional collage

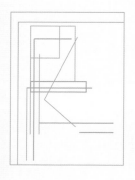

exhibit comparisons

Like many posters, this one for an exhibit of faculty work at a U.S. design school has few informational requirements. An event name, a date, a place, an emotional or visual appeal to the viewer, a conceptual message—these are the necessary components. Here, they are treated in a photographic collage of parts that likely echoes the design esthetic of the instructors' work, as well as provides interest and inspiration to the intended audience, in this case students of design and the fine arts.

Assembling specific parts of the information hierarchy, textures, and objects relating to the exhibit, the designers added and removed material as part of the collage process. The hierarchy is the basis for the organization of collage elements. Changing the placement and quality of textures, light and shadow changes the perceptual ordering of that hierarchy. In the series of sketches leading up to the final, it's clear how those changes led from flatter, more schematic presentations to a richer, luminous, more dimensional environment for the information.

Increased depth allowed the large-scale RISD to separate spatially from the other text and calls Faculty Biennial forward. The additional architecture of the exhibit's empirical information becomes sharper and more intricate as a foil to the loose, shadowy deformation of the background and surrounding elements.

project
Faculty Biennial
Exhibition poster
Offset lithography

client
**Rhode Island School
of Design**
Educational institution
Providence, RI

design
Skolos/Wedell
Canton, MA

Rhode Island School of Design
Museum of Art

Modular grid deconstruction on hierarchical grid

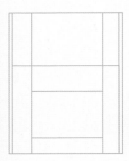

exhibit comparisons

01	04	17	18
21	26	31	
03	**07**	**12**	**15**
17	**21**	**34**	

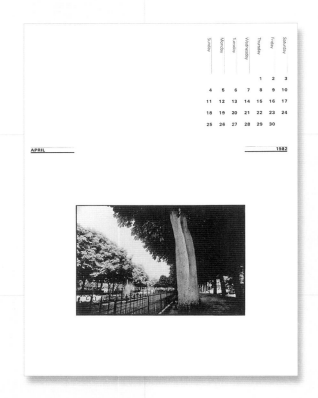

This calendar showcasing a photographer's images uses a simple predetermined structure to organize repeating elements, but is overlaid with a changing grid structure. On each page of the calendar, a symmetrical grid places the selected photograph, the name of the month, a marker for the year, and orientation alignments for the calendar grid above. The calendar grid itself expands and compresses or even reverses the relationship between its horizontal and vertical axes in response to the optical weights and compositional stresses within the photograph below it.

project
Calendar
Offset lithography
Duotone
Spiral bound at top

client
Friedrich Cantor
New York, NY

design
Willi Kunz Associates
New York, NY

photography
Friedrich Cantor
New York, NY

Sunday		7	14	21	28
Monday	1	8	15	22	29
Tuesday	2	9	16	23	30
Wednesday	3	10	17	24	
Thursday	4	11	18	25	
Friday	5	12	19	26	
Saturday	6	13	20	27	

NOVEMBER   **1982**

Sunday	1	8	15	22	29
Monday	2	9	16	23	30
Tuesday	3	10	17	24	31
Wednesday	4	11	18	25	
Thursday	5	12	19	26	
Friday	6	13	20	27	
Saturday	7	14	21	28	

AUGUST   **1982**

Sunday	Monday	Tuesday	Wednesday	Thursday	Friday	Saturday
					1	2
3	4	5	6	7	8	9
10	11	12	13	14	15	16
17	18	19	20	21	22	23
24	25	26	27	28	29	30
31						

JANUARY   **1982**

structure

Manuscript grid and column grid deconstruction

exhibit comparisons

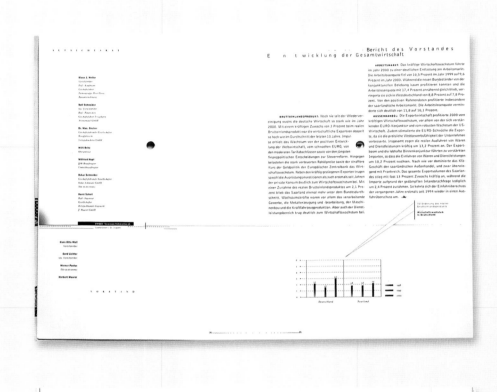

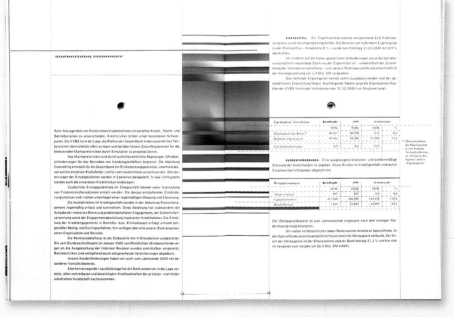

project
Annual report
Perfect bound book
with offset-printed wrapper
Text printed offset, two colors

client
Vereinigte Volksbanken
Financial services
Hof, Germany

design
Maksimovic & Partners
Ivica Maksimovic [CD]
Patrick Bittner [AD]
Saarbrucken, Germany

photography
Patrick Bittner
Andy Wakeford
Saarbrucken, Germany

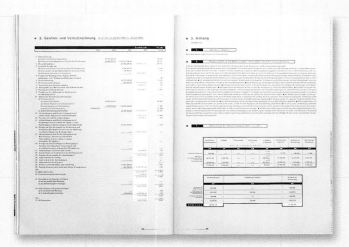

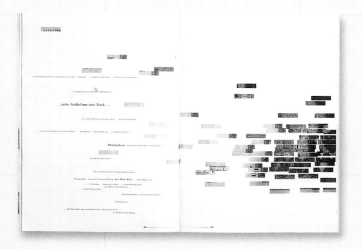

The delicate and detailed typographic treatments of this annual report for a German bank, some of which are deconstructions of printing details from money, stocks, and other financial documents, interact playfully with rigid columns. The column structure changes from section to section and is cut into or split apart as needed. Alternating justified manuscript- and two-column pages creates additional rhythm and a kind of unity that doesn't cramp the designer's intuitive impulses. The reader is allowed to enjoy the fine detailing of rules, dots, and diagrams.

Interestingly, the financial statements toward the back of the booklet are the least structured. Consolidated balance sheets span the full page in a more-or-less conventional numeric column structure, but subsequent pages break images and text apart into strips, as though being shredded.

By choosing an austere grid with intent to violate it on occasion, the designer creates a stately sense of tension between order and decoratively placed deconstructive detail.

structure

Hierarchic grid
with filmic collage
deconstruction

exhibit comparisons

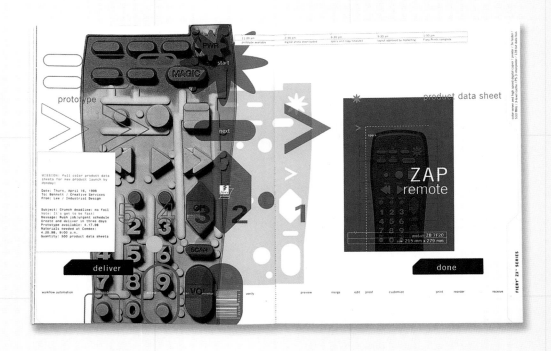

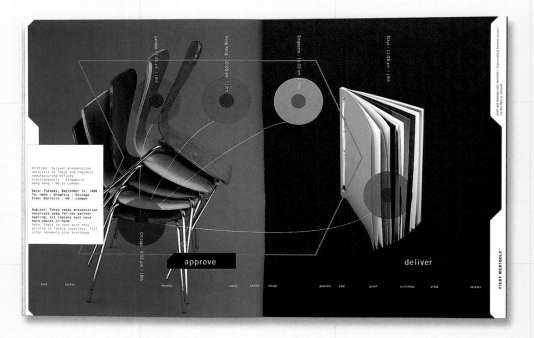

project	client	design	photography	illustration
Mission Possible Annual report *Perfect-bound book with printed-tissue jacket Offset lithography on uncoated text stock with plastic divider pages*	**Electronics for Imaging** Manufacturers of digital printing systems *San Mateo, CA*	**Tolleson Design** Steve Tolleson Jean Orlebeke *San Francisco, CA*	**Davies + Starr** *San Francisco, CA*	**Davies + Starr** *San Francisco, CA*

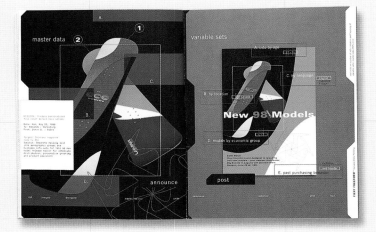

In this annual report for a manufacturer of high-end electronic printing technologies, several simple structures combine with dynamically composed imagery that invokes diagramming, electronic page headers, file folder tabs, and other office electronics vernacular in nongrid relationships.

The first section is a set of financial highlights, delivered in a very straight-forward text-block structure. Running text and simple graphs are set in bitmapped type and given ample margins and leading, yet without linear correspondence between baselines or hanglines. The focus becomes the text and the paper. Conceptually, the section takes on the aspect of a classified report, reflecting the project's thematic title.

The second section presents scenarios in which the client's technology makes nearly impossible electronic print jobs happen smoothly. This section follows its own structure, unrelated to that of the first: a home position for certain kinds of items, like a description of the scenario and key idea words, provides consistency against five photographic layouts that vary in complexity and treatment. Visual unity is given through details: dashed rules, type treatment, and geometric shapes.

The third section contains the financial data, again presented in a simple structure with tabs. In this section, however, the text column has been rotated, and its right margin corresponds to the text hangline from the first section.

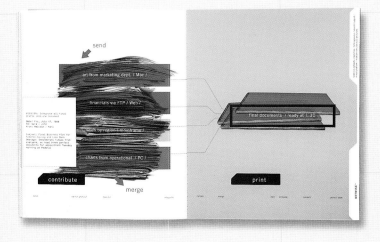

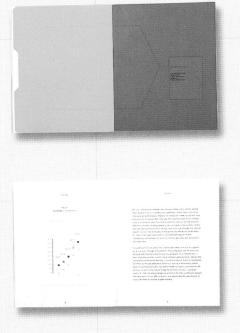

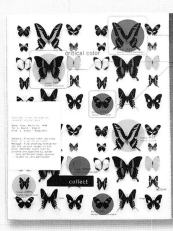

structure

Compound column grid deconstructed by collage

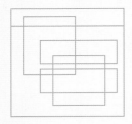

exhibit comparisons

04	05	07	09
10	14	16	19
22	23	24	26
28	30	34	
02	05	08	11
14	18	26	28
33			

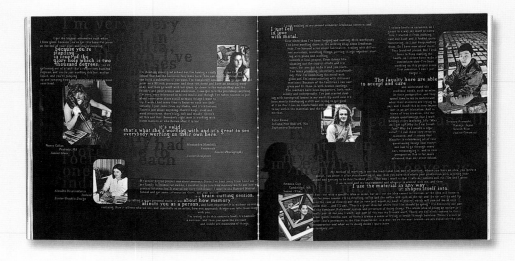

project
Course Catalog
Perfect-bound book
Offset lithography

client
Massachussetts College of Art
Educational institution
Boston, MA

design
Stoltze Design
Clifford Stoltze [AD]
Tracy Schroder
Heather Kramer
Peter Farrell
Resa Blatman
Boston, MA

photography
Cecilia Hirsch
Boston, MA

This course catalog relies on multiple structural ideas to convey the experimental, exploratory, and often antiestablishment environment of an art school. The overlap of images, type, and integration of several different alignment structures serves as a metaphor for the interaction of different artistic disciplines, as well as divorcing the institution from its counterparts: nonarts educational universities.

The first few spreads are seductively simple. Misalignments in the columns of the table of contents and the mission statement, while unorthodox, only hint at the upcoming dynamics. Beginning with the descriptive section about the surrounding city, each section takes on its own organizational qualities. Sometimes a few center-axis columns hang from the top of the page, sometimes there are no columns. Course information begins in a four-column structure but quickly dissolves, ignoring hanglines and, in some cases, running horizontally across the gutter of the spread.

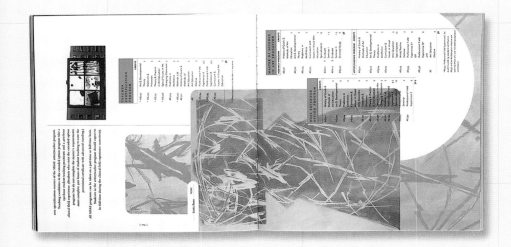

Photographs and artwork are arranged in non-rectangular boxes or are tinted behind running text. No consistent alignments, but the pages hold together in a clean, direct sort of tension where the visual qualities of the images and shapes are played against each other.

structure

Hierarchical grid deconstructed into multiple layers

exhibit comparisons

05	07	09	10
13	15	22	30
36			
04	08	14	18
20	23	31	32
34	36		

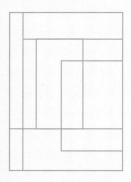

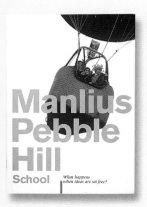

Manlius Pebble Hill School *What happens when ideas are set free?*

project
Admissions viewbook
Recruiting brochure
Saddle-stitched booklet
Offset lithography

client
Manlius Pebble Hill School
Private educational institution
Syracuse, NY

design
Timothy Samara
New York, NY

illustration
Timothy Samara
New York, NY

photography
Ron Trinca
Syracuse, NY

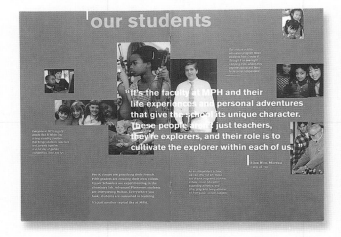

This admissions recruiting brochure for a private school focuses on positioning the school as a nexus in Western education—passing on the skills and knowledge associated with historic achievements as part of its curriculum, thereby preparing students to achieve greatness on their own. Each spread exhibits one Western achievement paired with a conceptually similar stage of student development: for example, early architecture becomes a metaphor for the kindergarten program. Each spread conforms to a hierarchical grid for specific features, but the remainder of the content is pushed around to accommodate the large drawings, photographs, and running text that are central to the concept.

Each event is catalogued in a vertically running bar of text at the left edge of the format, describing the event and giving pertinent information. The spread 'title' always runs across the center as a focal point, binding the elements together. Page numbers occupy a standard location at the lower right edge of the format. Column widths and type treatments remain consistent, but their relationship to each other, and to the format as a whole, change as needed to create a fluid composition with the photograph and drawing. Alignments overlap; texts are layered and cross the gutter.

A strictly informational student life section plays off these treatments but organically rearranges the grid elements—captions, quoted statements, inset pictures—based on their formal qualities alone.

Spontaneous hierarchical composition

exhibit comparisons

03	08	11	14
15	19	20	22
25	29	30	32
34			
04	09	19	22
23	27	30	34
36			

An intuitive hierarchical structure, based on the visual and conceptual qualities of a selected image, creates strong, concise branding across a series of posters for this Swiss arts festival. The designer conceived of the idea of radiology to represent the nature of the festival, which helps to illuminate the work of the normally underground community of up-and-coming artists. For the festival's first year, all of the relevant events were accessible by foot, so an X-ray of a foot was used. In the second year, some of the festival's venues could be reached by bus, so the image changed to that of a hand holding an overhead strap on a bus. Each year, the X-rayed object changes.

The information that clarifies the participants and venues is arranged based on pictorial details within or around the image, and so the structure of that information changes. The designer adjusts the position and treatment of the other two primary parts of the hierarchy, the festival title and the date block, in response to the overall composition for the image; type selection and prominence of the elements within the perceived hierarchy remains the same.

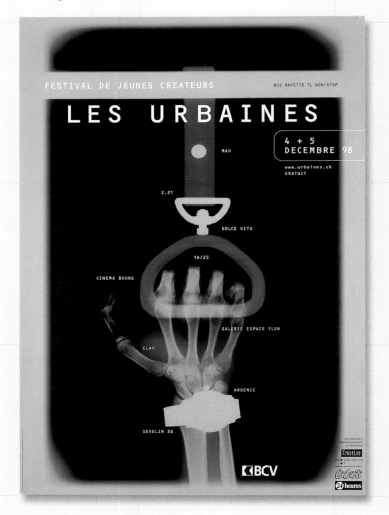

project
Underground Arts Festival
Promotional poster system
Offset lithography

client
Les Urbaines
Arts promotion organization
Lausanne, Switzerland

design
Atelier Poisson
Giorgio Pesce
Lausanne, Switzerland

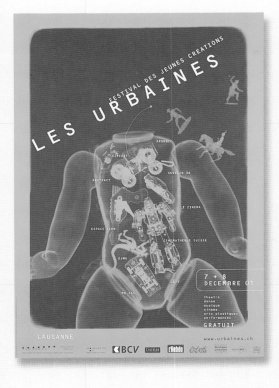

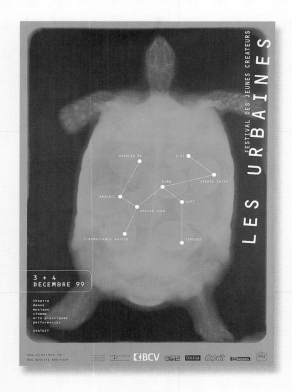

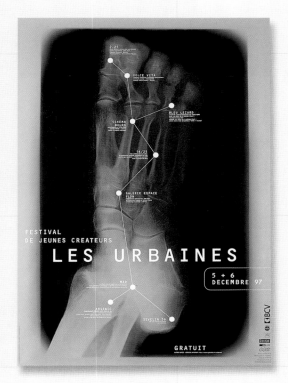

structure

Hierarchical grid deconstruction and decorative grid

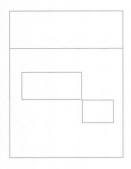

exhibit comparisons

In this annual report, the designers reversed the relationship between structure and illustration, grid and surface.

The concept section of the report focuses on statements that interact with a photograph of properties and property types relating to the company's real estate interests, and each spread is structurally completely different. Some ele-

ments, like boxed statements or quotes, charts, and small inset photographs, are repeated as treatments but follow no underlying structure, except for a single hangline that helps orient the reader from spread to spread. Otherwise, the elements move around freely, sometimes reacting to elements in the full-bleed photographs.

project
Real Places
Annual report
Perfect-bound book
Offset lithography

client
Pennsylvania Real Estate
Investment Trust
Philadelphia , PA

design
Allemann, Almquist & Jones
Philadelphia, PA

The backgrounds behind this antistructure,
however, are decorative patterns made of gridded
elements. The structural motif is appropriate to
the idea of square-footage or retail shopping
areas but acts as an illustration. The financial
statements defer to a standard two-colum grid
that subdivides as needed for tabular data.

structure

System of hierarchical compositions with collage and decorative modular grids

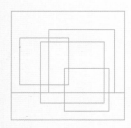

exhibit comparisons

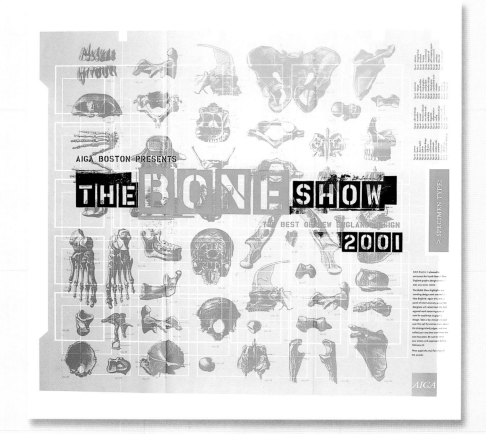

project
The BONE Show
Event identity system
Print collateral and
exhibition space
*Silkscreen and offset
(print collateral)
Wood, glass, vinyl lettering,
light projection (exhibition)*

client
**American Institute
of Graphic Arts, Boston
Chapter**
Professional designers'
association
Boston, MA

design
**Kristin Hughes
and Ink Design**
Poster

Kristin Hughes
all other applications
Pittsburgh, PA

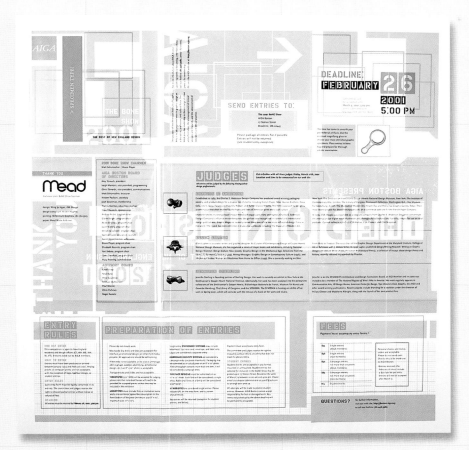

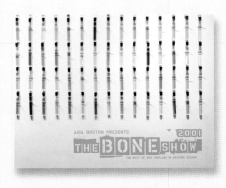

This branded system of promotional material, exhibition catalog, and exhibition uses a grid as the backdrop for its loose forensic/archaeological specimen metaphor. The visual texture of a grid binds all of the elements together, despite different textural qualities, reading directions, and collage-like overlays of information and decorative imagery.

The grid itself is reminiscent of the copy-camera positioning platform used to photograph items found in archaeological digs. Although it appears on every application, the grid doesn't function so much as an ordering system as a conceptual decoration. In some cases—the card and the certificate, for example—the grid is strictly texture. On the poster, its modules explode outward as an overlay that frames and dissects bone images, surprinted in silver. In the catalog, the module is made singular as a holding device for the exhibit information, but it doesn't exert any structural control over the information residing within it, other than to establish a left margin. Elements of the grid are consistently deformed and reused as needed; the system uses this inconsistency as part of its language.

Within the exhibit itself, the square module appears as pedestals supporting exhibited works, although the squares are arranged in a random way. Typographic elements are printed on translucent panels that interact across the gallery space with other typographic materials and images, making a three-dimensional reference to the flat printed language of the collateral material.

structure

**Optical composition
based on conceptual
criteria**

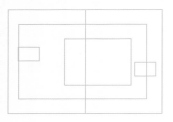

exhibit comparisons

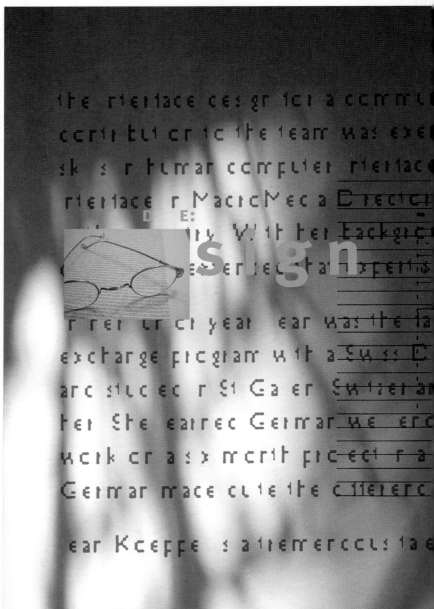

project
Design Issues
Periodical covers,
front and back

*Offset lithography in
two colors*

client
Design Issues
Trade journal for
designers

design
Dan Boyarski
Pittsburgh, PA

photography
Dan Boyarski
Pittsburgh, PA

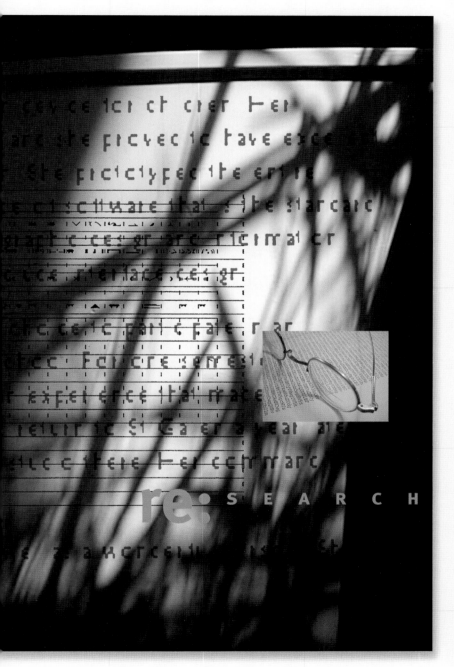

The organization of images and textures for this journal cover is optical and intuitive, based primarily on a desire to make connections between the image content and its textural qualities. The elements consist of deteriorating grids of type where the disintegration has rendered the language partially illegible, while enhancing its structural qualities; the strokes, the modular nature of the language, are visually more noticeable, but its function has been impaired. A play of light and shadow introduces depth but also references the idea of seeing with light aiding in the transmission of information through the eyes.

The insets play counterpoint to the background environment. Sharp photographs with clear depth of field contrast with the indistinct space of the background; conceptually, the reading glasses (symbolic of enhanced seeing) connect with the background image's illegible text. On each cover (front and back), the type is positioned in an intuitive relationship to the inset image, aligning along the edges or baseline to integrate it in to the overall composition.

Modular grid deconstruction

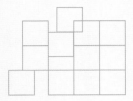

This spare and elegant suite of stationery for an urban florist explores the relation of geometric order to organic movement. Using the horizontal and vertical alignments of a simple modular grid as a starting point, the designers have shifted the modules around in reaction to the random, flowing movement of flowers. Some edges of the modules have been made visible, etched out as thin rules that align with or overlap other elements as needed.

The flowers seem to grow out from behind the grid, influencing its structure but also restating it in some places. Address and contact information are separated and allowed to float across partitions, but each informational item occupies a discreet area, as will the addressee's salutation and the letter that will eventually fill the lower portion of the page.

exhibit comparisons

02	06	12	19
26	31		
03	06	07	10
13	16	17	19
24	27	30	38

JAMIE ROTHSTEIN

distinctive floral designs

313 CHERRY STREET
PHILADELPHIA, PA 1 9 1 0 6

project
Corporate identity
Stationery system
Offset lithography

client
Jamie Rothstein
Distinctive Floral Designs
Floral designer
Philadelphia, PA

design
Mayer + Myers Design
Nancy Mayer [AD]
Greg Simmons
Philadelphia, PA

JAMIE ROTHSTEIN

distinctive floral designs

313 CHERRY STREET
PHILADELPHIA, PA 1 9 1 0 6

215 **238.1220**

JAMIE ROTHSTEIN

distinctive floral designs

313 CHERRY STREET
PHILADELPHIA, PA 1 9 1 0 6

215 **238.1220**

structure

Spontaneous hierarchical grid deconstruction

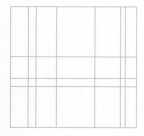

exhibit comparisons

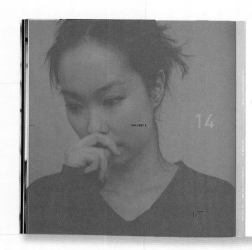

project
Art + Science
Promotional brochure
Perfect-bound book
Offset lithography with
metallic surprints and
translucent papers

client
Sandy Alexander Printers
Commercial printers
New York, NY

design
Ideas on Purpose
John E. Connolly
New York, NY

photography
Graham McIndoe
Chuck Shotwell
Pete McArthur
Alex Villaluz
Maria Robledo
New York, NY

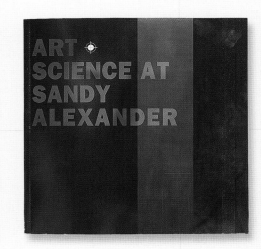

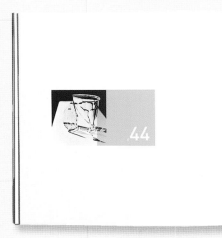

Four separate galleries of photographic reproduction form the primary
focus of this printer's showpiece. Each gallery section is devoted to
the work of a single photographer and designed around a given theme.
Structurally, alignment is minimal, and any alignment that exists is
violated in every other spread. Each gallery section relies on its own logic
to determine whether the alignments are articulated, but most often
the operating logic is optical.

On the divider pages, complementary texts alternate between contrasting
treatments based on the designer's sensitivity to the qualities of the type
in the format. The actual positioning of texts changes, but the same logic
applies to each occurrence. Centralized insets play off full-spread bleeds.
The structure of individual pages is wrapped up in contrasts of sequencing,
scale and color change, cropping and bleed, matte and reflective.

project
Lecture poster
Offset lithography

client
**American Center
for Design**
Arts institution
Chicago, IL

design
Bates Hori
Allen Hori
New York, NY

structure
**Architectonic
column grid
deconstruction**

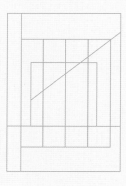

exhibit comparisons

project
Lecture poster
Offset lithography

client
**Princeton University
School of Architecture**
Educational institution
Princeton, NJ

design
Bates Hori
Allen Hori
New York, NY

In two individual posters—one a call for
entries to a design competition and the other
a lecture-series announcement—the designer
deploys a similar structure to organize the
presented material. Both posters contain a
centrally located rectangular area that acts
as a grounding point. In the call for entries,
that central area remains noticeably empty as
information slides around its perimeter; in
the lecture poster, the rectangular area houses
the most important conceptual information
and image. In each case, a predominantly
centered axis hints at a formal, symmetrical
system, but the symmetry is sidestepped by
diagrammatic or planar elements. Remnants
of column grids form informational sections
in each poster, but are overlaid with linear
elements, reduced to texture, or overlapped to
create a more complex and detailed surface.

structure

Nonorthogonal
grid deconstruction

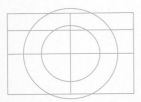

exhibit comparisons

03	06	08	10
25	31	35	
08	33		

A Broken Promise

Designed by Julie Carlini

Love is a dangerous thing.

The world is full of stories about people
who have defied convention, family
even death for love.

This is a story of a queen
who **betrayed** her people
and forever changed their nation
for the sake of love.

The visual representation of this spoken story is organized on a grid of concentric circles, rather than an orthogonal grid. The choice of the circle is conceptual, representing the cyclical aspect of life and the outward movement of the sound of a speaker's voice. The text moves around the outside of the primary circle that defines the spreads. As key phrases or words are delivered, they move into and through the circle, becoming augmented in size and motion. Subsequent text overlays previous text, giving continuity to the parts. The concentric rings of the grid create columns that are still visible, and which provide the same function as their conventional counterparts, separating thoughts and organizing passages into distinct parcels of information for accessibility.

project
A Broken Promise
Visual essay
Spiral-bound book
Black-and-white laserprints

school
Carnegie Mellon University
Educational institution
Pittsburgh, PA

design
Julie Saunders Carlini
Pittsburgh, PA
Karen Kornblum Berntsen, Professor

structure

Spontaneous geometric composition

exhibit comparisons

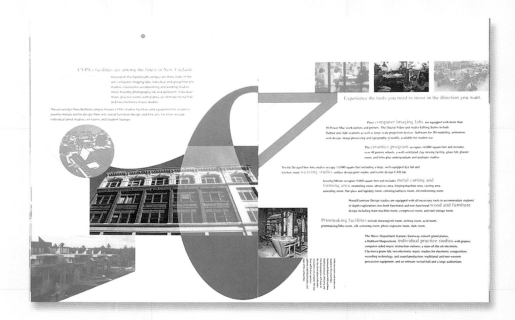

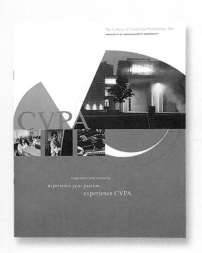

project
CVPA
Course catalog
Saddle-stitched booklet
Offset lithography in
four spot colors

client
UMASS Dartmouth
College of
Visual & Performing Arts
Educational institution
Boston, MA

design
Stoltze Design
Clifford Stoltze [AD]
Tammy Dotson
Boston, MA

photography
Cecilia Hirsch
Boston, MA

Clean geometric abstraction—semicircles, arcs, lines, and dots—and a fresh, unstudied approach to the composition of elements govern the layout of information for this brochure. Dramatic negative spaces surround and interact with clustered forms and freely composed units of typographic information in a "dance" around the format.

The information is accessible, despite its playful structure, because each part of the information is decisively located. Individual thoughts or components of information are separated from each other so the eye can access them easily.

Dynamic variation in the scale, shape, and proximity of elements creates a natural movement across the spreads, keeping the reader interested and helping to link successive paragraphs or ideas in an intuitive and easy-to-follow manner. This organizational method can be very successful when the informational requirements of the project are not too demanding.

structure

Modular grid deconstruction

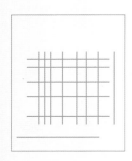

exhibit comparisons

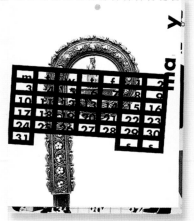

Addressing issues of construction, deconstruction, waste, and creation, this inventively produced calendar for a printing company prints its matrix on top of recycled printed matter. Each month's calendar matrix pushes and pulls at the underlying grid structure that displays the days and weeks. In some cases, the intervals between the modules in the matrix are compressed and expanded. A secondary logic, involving a superimposed grid of geometric elements, interacts with the typography, alternately building shapes around it or obscuring it under invisible forms. The individual months and their deconstructions gain added meaning in the context of the preexisting printed image underneath it.

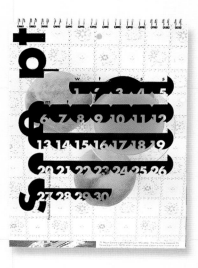

project
Recycled calendar
Self promotion
Wire-O bound
Black-and-white laserprints
on offset-printed make-
ready sheets

client
Praxis
Graphic designers
Los Angeles, CA

design
Praxis
Simon Johnston
Los Angeles, CA

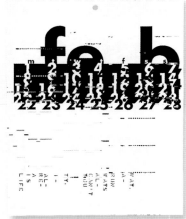

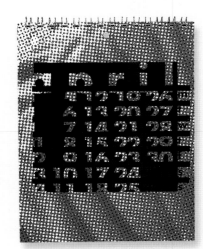

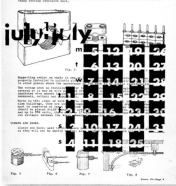

structure

**Pictorial
manuscript grid
deconstruction**

exhibit comparisons

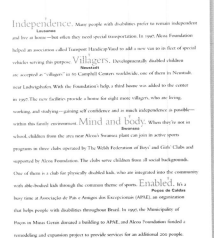

Our day begins in this ancient Hungarian city, once the crowning site **Szekesfehervar** of kings, known in Roman times as Alba Regia. Today, its people are growing their industry, building a future, and grappling with problems known to cities the world over. In several such efforts, Alcoa Foundation was able to help in 1997. → With equipment and furniture for eight rooms of the Crisis Management Center (Krizskezelo Otthon), providing housing, hot meals, financial assistance, medical attention, and social support for the homeless. → A minivan for the Frim Jakab Specialized Ability Development Home, to transport children with multiple handicaps. → Arthroscopic, ultrasound, and ambulance equipment for the Szent Gyorgy Regional Hospital of Fejer County. → Costumes and instruments for the pride of Szekesfehervar, the Alba Regia folkdance group, which performs Hungarian folk music and dance in the city, throughout Europe, and in North Africa and Canada. → A copper relief portrait of Coloman Beauclerk, King of Hungary from 1095 to 1116, to become a permanent exhibit at the Saint Istvan Royal Museum. → Computer equipment for the Metallurgical and Electrical Engineering departments of the University of Miskolc. → Water quality control and wastewater laboratory equipment in the School of Environmental Engineering at the University of Veszprum. → Computer equipment for science and engineering students at the Technical University of Budapest, and for Business Economics majors at the Budapest University of Economic Sciences.

Independence. Many people with disabilities prefer to remain independent **Lausanne** and live at home—but often they need special transportation. In 1997, Alcoa Foundation helped an association called Transport Handicap Vaud to add a new van to its fleet of special vehicles serving this purpose. Villagers. Developmentally disabled children **Neustadt** are accepted as "villagers" in 89 Camphill Centers worldwide, one of them in Neustadt, near Ludwigshafen. With the Foundation's help, a third home was added to the center in 1997. The new facilities provide a home for eight more villagers, who are living, working, and studying—gaining self confidence and as much independence as possible— within this family environment. Mind and body. When they're not in **Swansea** school, children from the area near Alcoa's Swansea plant can join in active sports programs in three clubs operated by The Welsh Federation of Boys' and Girls' Clubs and supported by Alcoa Foundation. The clubs serve children from all social backgrounds. One of them is a club for physically disabled kids, who are integrated into the community with able-bodied kids through the common theme of sports. Enabled. It's a **Poços de Caldas** busy time at Associação de Pais e Amigos dos Excepcionais (APAE), an organization that helps people with disabilities throughout Brazil. In 1997, the Municipality of Poços in Minas Gerais donated a building to APAE, and Alcoa Foundation funded a remodeling and expansion project to provide services for an additional 200 people.

VANCOUVER

project
Annual report
Perfect-bound book
Offset lithography

client
Alcoa Foundation
Corporate philanthropic
organization
Pittsburgh, PA

design
**Landesberg Design
Associates**
Rick Landesberg
Karen Kornblum Berntsen
Pittsburgh, PA

Although this elegant annual report uses a conventional column grid for its financial disclosures and management information, its front matter has almost no structure at all.

A single hangline that orients the running text is the only alignment present; the flush-left alignment at the left margin of the pages is so close to the edge of the format that the text almost appears to flow in from outside the book. This single horizontal flowline establishes a clear headspace at the top of the page into which some illustrative material is placed, but the organization of the pages is dependent on the rhythm of the running text. Occasional callouts of key words or phrases and a diagram of the sun traveling in the sky at particular times link the text conceptually to a sense of place and time on the Earth. The horizontal line establishes a sense of horizon, which is perhaps seen from the ocean—a design element referenced in the linear wave of text across the pages. On the image spreads that alternate with the text spreads, a simple visual relationship between the arc of the sun and a full-bleed image grounds the reader.

structure

Collage and filmic column grid deconstruction

exhibit comparisons

project
Something from Nothing
Design monograph
Case-bound book
Offset lithography

client
RotoVision Publishing
Publishers
East Sussex, England

design
April Greiman
Los Angeles, CA

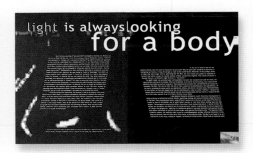

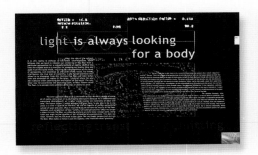

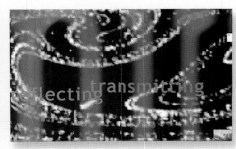

The organization of this book, both verbally and visually, is filmic in nature: each spread is a frame that refers to the one preceding it and sets up the next. A minimal set of constants—outer margin, page number, folio, and inset at the lower-right corner—holds a loosely defined column structure in place from page to page. The number of columns, their widths, and the size of type within them change as appropriate, in relation to the imagery on the page.

The relationships between images and typography are intuitive: the overall logic of the page spreads is visually off the cuff, an immediate response to the quantity of text, the predominant shapes in the background image, and how these meld to form a cohesive composition.

Spreads are set up as sequences of interconnected visual ideas. The negative space in an image on a given spread may yield to a similarly shaped positive image on the next; an inset or background image in the spread following that may be enlarged to a full-bleed image that crosses over onto a subsequent spread. Continuity is created through rhythmic, spatial interconnection between pages.

structure

Spontaneous geometric composition

exhibit comparisons

Intersecting diagonals and sharp angular movements, derived from the juxtaposition of photographic and typographic line elements, create a dynamic organization for the imagery and information in this poster. The designer uses the vertical diagonal of the crane arm and the sudden angle of the overhead street lamp to both disorient the viewer and provide a primary superstructure for the poster. The typography moves upward and outward, with positions for each line determined in part by the superstructure. At the same time, the designer counters the tumult with subtle alignments and focal points: The airplane at lower left anchors the composition and creates an optical alignment between lines of information that echo the direction of the superstructure.

project
LIFT
Promotional poster
Offset lithography

client
LIFT
London International
Festival of Theatre
London, England

design
Frost Design
Vincent Frost
Sonya Dyokava
London, England

photography
Nick Higgins
London, England

structure

Systematic collage column grid deconstruction

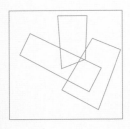

exhibit comparisons

03	05	06	07
09	13	15	16
25	28	31	33
36	37		
02	05	08	14
18	26	28	33

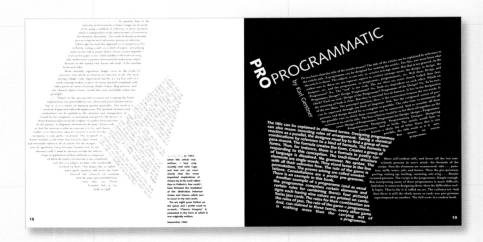

Organized around the principle of collage, this inventive design journal walks a middle ground between apparent chaos and order. Careful study of cut-paper shapes and their overlaps led to the development of a system for laying out paragraphs of text. A comprehensive design manual provides guidelines for creating the shapes of the text boxes. Reading order depends on a number of variables: the relative position of the collage shapes, the size and orientation of the text within those shapes, and the density of the text on the page. By varying these parameters, the designer is able to control flow through the paragraphs when needed.

The system allows for a great deal of control and a great deal of potential for discovering new organizational methods for text and image.

project
Cut & Paste
Design journal
Black-and-white laserprints
Spiral binding

school
Rhode Island School of Design
Providence, RI

design
Andrea Vazquez
Tom Ockerse, instructor

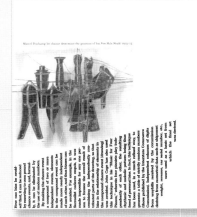
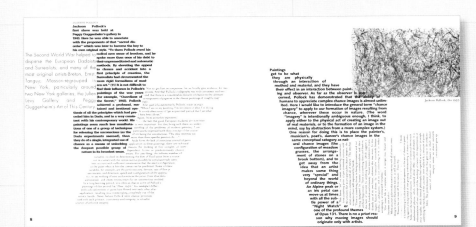
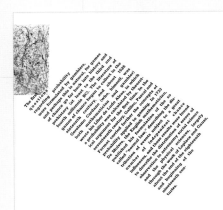

structure

Compound modular/ column grid integrated with collage

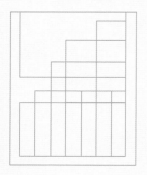

exhibit comparisons

project
**Academic calendar and
student handbook**
Saddle-stitched book
Offset lithography

client
University of the Arts
Educational institution
Philadelphia, PA

design
Mayer + Myers Design
Nancy Mayer [AD]
Kim Mollo
George Plesko
Greg Simmons
Alexandra Well
Philadelphia, PA

The calendar and student handbook for this art school wrap a conventionally grid-based calendar and column structure with a free-form collage of elements in the calendar pages.

The column-structure of the informational sections is made clear in the table of contents, but the loose, nongrid composition of the months is hinted at in the content's title area at the top of the spread. The contents listing and corollary information jump up and down off the five columns below, and alignments within that area begin to slip horizontally as well.

For each month of the academic year, a famous local artist is featured in a multilayered collage of type, image, and geometric stepping that integrates this free composition with the calendar grid below. Captions within the collage follow a standard stylistic treatment in terms of font selection, size, and left-flush alignment, but their placement is part of the collage logic surrounding it. The name of each respective month is set in a bold, dimensional construction that provides a visual transition between the collage and the modular grid. The handbook section returns to a regular five-column grid.

structure

Geometric pictorial allusion

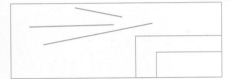

exhibit comparisons

project
Invitation
Auction preview reception
Offset lithography

client
Christie's Auction House
Auctioneers of art and
fine estates
New York, NY

design
**Christie's Creative
Services**
Lynn Fylak
New York, NY

photography
**Christie's Creative
Services**
New York, NY

Marcia Hobbs, Chairman, Christie's Los Angeles

Neal Meltzer, Director of Contemporary Art, Christie's New York

Deborah McLeod, Senior Specialist, Contemporary Art, Christie's Los Angeles

request the pleasure of your company at
a reception and private viewing of
Highlights from Christie's Fall Sale of Contemporary Art
including property from the

ESTATE OF JOHN M. AND MARION A. SHEA

cover
Alexander Calder
Aspen, 1948
(detail)

Monday, October 6, 1997
6:00 pm – 8:00 pm

Christie's
360 North Camden Drive
Beverly Hills

R.s.v.p
(310) 385 2662

Valet
Parking

Property will be offered at Christie's New York on November 18 and 19, 1997

The typographic handling of this invitation's interior is
based on the art selected for reproduction on its cover—
a mobile by Alexander Calder that is a highlight of the
reception being announced by the card.

The simple geometry of the mobile is further reduced
to planar abstraction in the way it is cropped on the
invitation's cover; the type inside plays off its diagonals,
against a red dictated by the mobile's painted struts.
The uppermost lines of type teeter whimsically over the
precariously balanced text below it in a clear reference
to Calder's mobile construction.

structure

Spontaneous architectonic composition

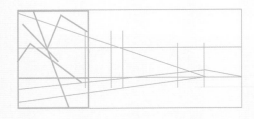

exhibit comparisons

project
A New Era of Excellence
Event invitation
Offset lithography

client
**University of
Pennsylvania Graduate
School of Education**
Educational institution
Philadelphia, PA

design
Paone Design Associates
Gregory Paone
Philadelphia, PA

photography
Trevor Dixon
Philadelphia, PA

The invitation for an event celebrating a renovated university building uses a montage of the building's architecture as a main compositional influence.

The type is subservient to the formal dynamism of the building's angular construction and its organization on the page. Intersecting translucent planes overlay similarly luminous architectural elements in a shifting temporal space; the typography takes some cues from the architecture (most notably on the cover) but remains spare, condensing down to a single line that travels succinctly across the interior. The event program reiterates the main compositional idea on its front side but defers to an ordered column structure on the reverse.

structure

Spontaneous architectonic composition

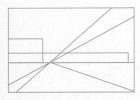

exhibit comparisons

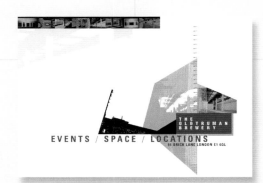

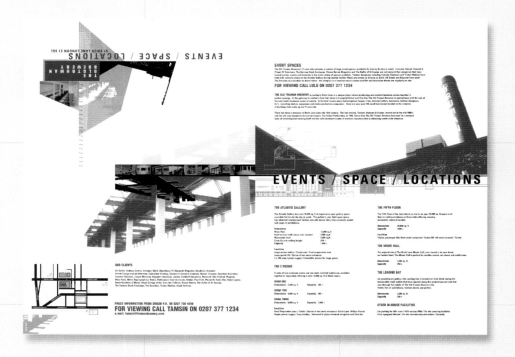

Each surface of this poster/flyer advertising a building redevelopment in London is organized around a hard-edged composition of the building's architectural elements.

project
Promotional poster
Offset lithography

client
Old Truman Brewery
Offices and event location
development
London, England

design
Insect
Paul Humphrey
Luke Davies
London, England

Typography is integrated along the various diagonal and horizontal axes defined by the compositions.

In particular, the front side of the poster is extremely dynamic, with promotional, as well as strictly informational, typography running across angular cuts in multiple perspectives. A conceptual horizon line orients the reader to a sense of three-dimensional space. The reverse presents similar architectonic constructions, but the type settles down into a more conventional column structure.

structure

**Relational-scale
information
architecture**

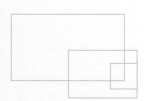

exhibit comparisons

07	08	11	17
28			
07	25	33	38

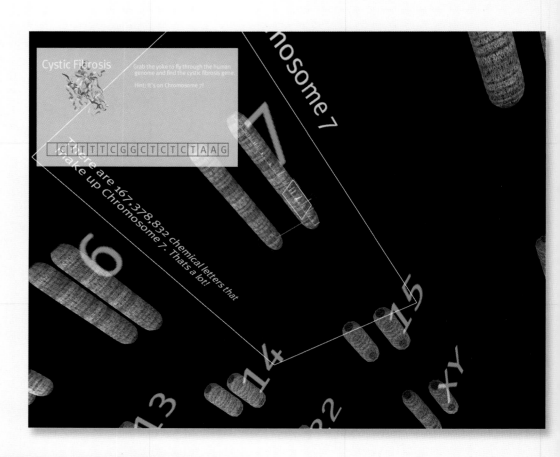

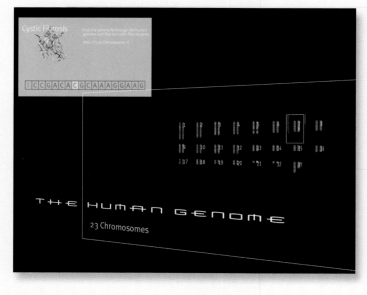

By communicating extremely complex information
in an intuitive way, this dynamically spatial interface
for a computer-generated map of the human genome
organizes information in virtual space based on the
natural shapes of the biological material. Instead
of imposing a modular structure to contain the
information, the designer uses the existing genetic
architecture as the information structure. Viewers
are able to move into, through, and around the components of genetic material.

project
**Human Genome
Interactive**
User interface
©2001
Small Design Firm, Inc.

client
**Museum of Science and
Industry**
Educational museum
Chicago, IL

design
Small Design Firm
David Small
Cambridge, MA

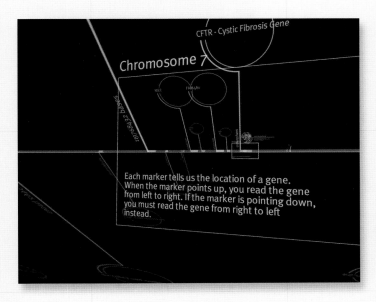

From an exterior specimen view of the chromo-
somes, laid out into rows, the user can intuitively
point to the chromosome they'd like explore, and
in doing so, fly into it for closer inspection. Within
this enlarged view, the user can choose from additional components that have become visible. Their
position is relative to the superstructure, of which
they are a part. Diagrammatic information and
text are positioned in relation to the structures
they describe.

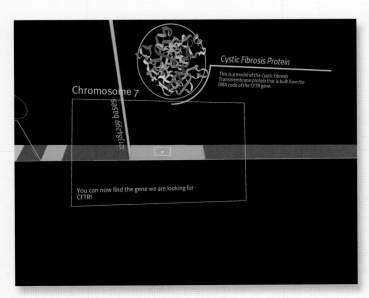

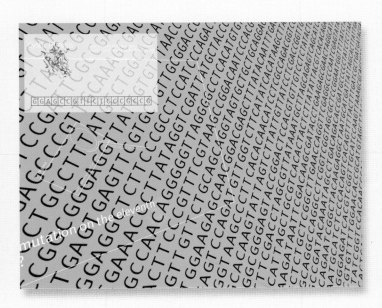

At the upper left of the screen, a navigational
box shows relative position within the structure
and highlights information relevant to that
location.

structure

Spontaneous optical column-grid deconstruction

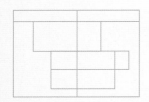

DAVID A HUGHES & JOHN MURPHY
COMPOSERS

After successful solo careers, Hughes and Murphy first collaborated on the cinematic score for 'Leon the Pig Farmer'. They announced their arrival among the finest British film composers with their music for 'Lock Stock and Two Smoking Barrels', but their versatile talents have been heard on a host of other films including, 'Solitaire for Two', 'The Real Howard Spitz', 'Stiff Upper Lips' and 'Giving Tongue'. They have also scored 'The Valley - Kosovo' and 'Horny - Tube Tales'. Recently listed in Variety's 'top 50 talents to watch', they have just completed their third Hollywood studio film soundtrack. **One More Kiss** is their 5th collaboration with director Vadim Jean.

'An ambitious, strikingly shot love story. An ode to life.'
Variety

'Set against the austere beauty of Scotland, One More Kiss is quite wonderful to look at and easily director Jean's most cinematic film to date.
Despite its themes, surprisingly life-affirming, with a sincere and moving message which should inspire all those who see it.'
Empire January 2000

'A fine cast and a fine story that lingers as long as a lover's first kiss.'
Film Review February 2000

'After the London [Film Festival] screening an elderly woman who used to be an actress, rushed up to her to add congratulations and told her: 'You know dear, you have just done something I was never able to do; make a whole cinema cry.'
Interview with Valerie Edmond in The Sunday Herald 26/12/'99

'Director Jean sets up a great dilemma: should Sam's wife be generous or give in to jealousy? Is their relationship strong enough to survive Sarah's reappearance. Edmond, gives a wonderfully unsentimental performance.
You're torn between horror and envy at Sarah's frankness. But the actress reminds us, 'If she were a man, would her behaviour be so shocking?' A terrific date movie - you'll come out arguing for days.'
Woman's Journal - Film of the month. February 2000

'A beautiful film... A must see for anyone with a heart.'
John Millar, Sunday Mail

MUSIC

Silva Screen Records is one of the most renowned names in film music. With over 500 albums released worldwide over the past ten years the breadth of repertoire has now expanded to include World, Contemporary Jazz, Rock, Classical, Opera, Original Soundtracks and New Recordings of Classic Film and TV Music. Silva Screen currently has some 200 soundtrack titles in their catalogue with recent releases including 'A Simple Plan', 'Hideous Kinky', 'Bond Back in Action', 'Raise the Titanic' and '8mm'.

AMOR TI VIETA
Performed by Tito Beltran
courtesy of Silva Screen Records

WHERE DO YOU GO TO MY LOVELY?
Performed by Peter Sarstedt
courtesy of EMI Records

AVE MARIA
Performed by Slava
courtesy of Victor Entertainment

ROSES FROM THE SOUTH
Performed by The Royal Philharmonic Orchestra
courtesy of Zomba

BEAUTIFUL DREAMER
Performed by James Cosmo, One More Kiss Ltd

YOU, FASCINATING YOU
Performed by Connie Lush
courtesy of Pasquale Frustaci

SWIMMERS
Performed by Milo
courtesy of Pumpkin Music Ltd

HEY BOY, HEY GIRL
Performed by Louis Prima and Keely Smith
courtesy of Capitol Records and Warner-Chappell

CARUSO
Performed by Julian Jensen
courtesy of BMG Publishing

THROUGH THE RAIN
Performed by Gavin Clarke
courtesy of Independiente Ltd

HOW ABOUT YOU?
Performed by Connie Lush
courtesy of EMI

SOUNDTRACK AVAILABLE ON SILVASCREEN RECORDS.

---

exhibit comparisons

04 05 07 09

10 15 16 24

25 31 34

02 05 08 11

14 18 26 28

33 37

Using a series of staggered, truncated, and shifting columns, the designers integrate typography and image to suggest the backdrop of the film this booklet promotes, New York City. Relatively straightforward columns of old-style serif type overlap each other, and the overlap is exploited as an opportunity to create architectural shapes for the type, which is reminiscent of buildings.

The columns become another architectural component of the montage of photographic elements that also depict the city. The shifts between column areas are carefully controlled so that conventional reading order is generally maintained; a rhythmic, left-to-right movement is preserved through the shapes of the columns, outdents, and indents. Linear elements add further clarification and connect information across the gutters, as well as suggest the travel component of the film's subject.

project
One More Kiss
Film marketing booklet
Offset lithography

client
Freewheel International
Mob Films
Jam Pictures
London, England

design
Why Not Associates
London, England

SHORT SYNOPSIS

When Sarah Hopson realises her successful high-rise
New York lifestyle is devoid of meaning, she packs her
bags and heads for her home town in the Scottish Borders
to look for Sam, her childhood sweetheart and the only
man she ever loved.

Sam Murray runs a restaurant. He and Sarah grew
up together and Sam hoped they'd grow old together.
His world fell apart the day Sarah left and now she's back;
standing on his doorstep telling him she'd like to spend
some time with him, to turn his life inside out all over
again. He introduces her to his wife Charlotte and explains
that now, his time belongs to someone else. Sarah leaves the restaurant dejected and returns to the house where
she grew up, where her father still lives. Not that he wants to see her. Frank has been
sitting in the same arm chair for the last seven years and doesn't particularly want to
get out of it. Not for anybody. Not until his daughter tells him why she's back.
One More Kiss is a story about rediscovering love and how when
perceptions are forced to change, life can hold an entirely
different meaning.

CAST

Sam	Gerard Butler
Frank	James Cosmo
Sarah	Valerie Edmond
Charlotte	Valerie Gogan
Jude	Danny Nussbaum
Barry	Carl Proctor

CREW

Director	Vadim Jean
Producers	Vadim Jean
	Paul Brooks
Co Producers	Jane Walmsley & Michael Braham
Executive Producers	Derek Roy & Sara Giles
Writer	Suzie Halewood
Casting	Carl Proctor
Director of Photography	Mike Fox
Focus	Matt Fox
Loader	Ant Hugill
Editor	Joe McNally
Assistant Editor	Stine Goetric
Line Producer	Ian Sharples
Production Co-ordinator	Natalie Sinclair
Production Designer	Simon Hicks
Art Director	Louise Bedford
Sound Recordists	Mike Lax
	Tommy Hair
Make-Up & Hair Design	Colette King
Costume Designer	Linda Brooker
Continuity	Shelley Kieley
Sound Editor	Ian Wilson
Composers	John Murphy & David A Hughes
Dialogue Editor	Keith Tunney
Dubbing Mixer	Tim Alban
Catering	Simon Tickner
Runners	Jon Brooke
	Sam Stonehill
	Jim Manningham
	Graham Spence

PAUL BROOKS
PRODUCER

After a degree in philosophy and literature at London University, Paul Brooks started
his business life in property. He made a leap into films through his role as executive
producer on 'Leon the Pig Farmer' in 1992. Since then, he has produced or executive produced ten feature films, including
'Solitaire for Two', 'Clockwork Mice', 'Killing Time', 'Darklands' and 'The Real Howard
Spitz'. He was the founder and chairman of Metrodome Distribution and has served
on the government's Middleton Committee on film.

Whilst at Metrodome, Paul commissioned the
script for One More Kiss. He has just completed 'Shadow
of the Vampire' as executive producer for Nicolas Cage's
production company, Saturn, starring John Malkovich
and Willem Dafoe.

FREEWHEEL INTERNATIONAL
EXECUTIVE PRODUCERS

Freewheel International are well established as film
pre-production financiers but, impressed by the script and
the project as a whole, decided to make One More Kiss their
first venture into production finance.

JAM PICTURES
CO-PRODUCERS

JAM Pictures was formed in 1996 to produce drama for
film, TV and stage. JAM Pictures' principals, both highly
experienced independent producers, are Jane Walmsley
and Michael Braham. Jane has completed numerous award-
winning documentaries and features for the BBC, ITV,
Channel 4, satellite stations, America's Discovery Channel
and ABC Australia. Michael has been responsible
for a number of dramas, including 'Spender', the top-rating crime series with Jimmy
Nail, for BBC Television and 'The Hawk', a psychological thriller starring Helen Mirren
for Channel 4 Films.

JOE McNALLY
EDITOR

Working predominantly on commercials for TV, Joe has worked with many top UK
production companies and advertising agencies. In 1997 he set up his own editing company 'Joe Cuts'
and continued to work on campaigns including New Deal
Welfare to Work, Nissan Primera Eyes, Bupa and Esso.
One More Kiss is his first feature film.

MIKE FOX
DIRECTOR OF PHOTOGRAPHY

Mike Fox started in the film industry as a projectionist
at the Royalty Cinema in Bowness. He has worked in
the industry for thirty-three years starting as assistant
cameraman on 'Disappearing World' and 'World at War'
before moving up to director of photography. He then
worked on several series and single dramas before making
three films with Alan Bennett. He has won several awards,
most notably the New York Festival Gold for 'Lost Children
of the Empire' and the BBC Bristol TV award for 'Breaking
Through'. In the 90's he moved into mainstream documentary, filming 'Around Whicker's World',
'Coltrane in a Cadillac', 'In the Wild Lions' with Anthony Hopkins and the award winning
'Black Daisies for the Bride'.

structure

Diagram, collage, and compound column-grid deconstructions

exhibit comparisons

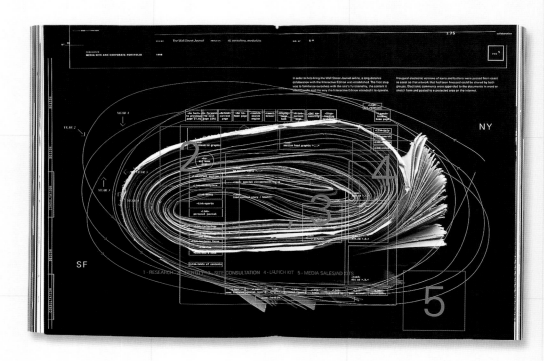

This complex overview of a design studio's work process and personality defies the conventional catalog structure that one might normally use to organize a vast amount of exhibited material. Instead of a repetitive structure that accommodates all different kinds of presentation, the designers change the presentation structure depending on a number of variables: the nature of the project being exhibited, the components being shown on a given spread, and the creative process that the designers want to highlight. Each project, therefore, is given a completely individual context and energy, and this is appropriate to the conceptual approach that the design firm is trying to make clear.

An important part of the organizational method, however, is the integration of graphic elements, process diagrams and type related to the actual project in a section. These devices surround, overlay, and tie together individual images of each project as the designer intuits: sometimes portions of the client brief and diagrams are used to show thinking, sometimes complex images are given more white space to compensate for complexity, and sometimes more simple images are joined with relevant linear or textural elements. All projects share a set of navigational devices at the top of the spread that indicates the project name and number, the client, and the project type.

project
Soak Wash Rinse Spin
Design monograph
*Paperback bound in
plastic jacket*
Offset lithography

client
Tolleson Design
San Francisco, CA

**Princeton Architectural
Press**
Princeton, NJ

design
Tolleson Design
Steve Tolleson [AD]
San Francisco, CA

photography
Tony Stromberg
San Francisco, CA

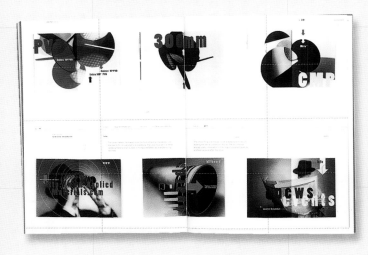

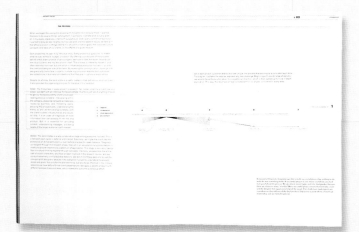

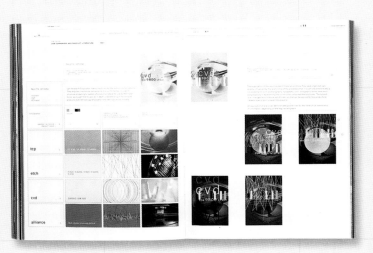

Index of Contributors

30 | 12

Willi Kunz Associates, Inc.
2112 Broadway, Rm. 500
New York, NY 10023
wkany@aol.com

27

Landesberg Design
1219 Bingham Street
Pittsburgh, PA 15203
www.landesbergdesign.com

09 | 07

Level Design
141 West 28th Street, Suite 6B
New York, NY 10001
www.levelnyc.com

13

Maksimovic & Partners
Johannisstraße 5
66111 Saarbrücken
Germany
www.maksimovic.de

21 | 31

Mayer & Myers
619 South Tenth Street
Philadelphia, PA 19147
www.mayerandmyers.com

01

McCoy & McCoy
mccoykj@id.iit.edu

24

MetaDesign AG
Bergmannstrasse 102
10961 Berlin
Germany
www.metadesign.com

20 | 31

Meta Design SF
350 Pacific Avenue, 3rd Floor
San Francisco, CA 94111
www.metadesign.com

28 | 06

Thomas Ockerse
37 Woodbury Street
Providence, RI 02906
tockerse@brainiac.com

04 | 17 | 09 | 33

Paone Design Associates, Ltd.
Saint Patrick's Schoolhouse
242 South Twentieth Street, 3rd Floor
Philadelphia, PA 19103-5602
www.paonedesign.com

34

Pentagram UK
11 Needham Road
London W11 2RP
England
www.pentagram.com

10

Pettistudio LLC
55 Washington Street, Suite 551
Brooklyn, NY 11201
www.pettistudio.com

23 | 17

Atelier Poisson
Place de L'Europe 8
1003 Lausanne
Switzerland

13 | 19 | 35

Poulin + Morris
286 Spring Street, 6th Floor
New York, NY 10013
www.poulinmorris.com

02 | 26

Praxis *Simon Johnston*
254 Tranquillo Road
Pacific Palisades, CA 90272
prxs_dsgn@aol.com

16

Timothy Samara
436 West 22nd Street
New York, NY 10011
timsamara@hotmail.com

27 | 11

Skolos-Wedell, Inc.
125 Green Street
Canton, MA 02021
www.skolos-wedell.com

33 | 38 | 35

Small Design Firm, Inc.
75 Massachusetts Avenue, Suite 11
Cambridge, MA 02139 - 3070
www.davidsmall.com

Index of Contributors *continued*

15 | 25

Stoltze Design
49 Melcher Street
Boston, MA 02210
www.stoltze.com

21 | 14 | 37

Tolleson Design
220 Jackson Street, Suite No. 310
San Francisco, CA 94111
www.tolleson.com

06 | 03

Niklaus Troxler Design
P.O. Box
CH 6130 Willisau
Switzerland
www.troxlerart.ch

05 | 14

UNA (amsterdam) Designers
Mauritskade 55
1092 AD Amsterdam
Netherlands
www.unadesigners.nl

30

Andrea Vazquez
Rhode Island School of Design
Two College Street
Providence, RI 02903
www.risd.edu

29

Vignelli Associates
130 East 67th Street
New York, NY 10018
www.vignelli.com

03 | 05 | 36

Why Not Associates
22C Shepherdess Walk
London N1 7LB
England
www.whynotassociates.com

Additional contributors

David Carson *pp. 118,119, 121, 125*
414 Broadway
New York, NY 10013
www.davidcarsondesign.com

Jenny Chan *pp. 122, 123*
55 Jackson Road
Hamden, CT 06517

Sheila deBretteville *p. 28*
Yale University School of Art
New Haven, CT 06511
www.yale.edu

Enterprise IG *p.21*
570 Lexington Avenue, 5th Floor
New York, NY 10022
www.enterpriseig.com

Total Design *p.20*
Paalbergweg 42
1105 BV Amsterdam
Netherlands
www.totaldesign.nl

Wolfgang Weingart *pp. 115, 116*
Hochschule für Gestaltung und Kunst
Typography Department, G_102
Vogelsangstrasse 15
CH 4058 Basel
Switzerland

Kristie Williams *pp. 122, 123*
University of the Arts
Department of Graphic Design
333 South Broad Street
Philadelphia, PA 19103
www.uarts.edu

Bibliography

Aicher, Otl.
World as Design. NP: VCH Publications, 1994.

Aldersey-Williams, Hugh et al.
Cranbrook Design: The New Discourse. New York: Rizzoli, 1990.

Aldersey-Williams, Hugh.
New American Design. New York: Rizzoli, 1988.

Bayer, Herbert; Gropius, Walter; and Gropius, Ise, editors.
Bauhaus 1919–1928. New York: The Museum of Modern Art, 1938.

Bosshard, Hans Rudolf.
The Typographic Grid. Sulgen/Zurich: Niggli AG, 2000.

Buddensieg, Tilmann.
Industrialkultur: Peter Behrens and the AEG. Cambridge, MA: MIT Press, 1984.

Celant, Germano, et al.
Design: Vignelli. New York: Rizzoli, 1990

Dickerman, Leah, editor.
Building the Collective: Soviet Graphic Design 1917-1937; Selections from the Merrill C. Berman Collection. New York: Princeton Architectural Press, 1996..

Doig, Allan.
Theo Van Doesburg: Painting into Architecture, Theory into Practice. Cambridge: Cambridge University Press, 1986.

Gerstner, Karl.
Designing Programmes. Teufen AR, Switzerland: Arthur Niggli, 1968.

Hoffmann, Armin.
Armin Hoffmann: His Work, Quest and Philosophy. Basel, Boston, Berlin: Birkhauser Verlag, 1989.

Kunz, Willi.
Typography: Macro- and Micro-aesthetics. Teufen, Switzerland: Verlag Arthur Niggli, 1999.

Lupton, Elaine.
Mixing Messages: Graphic Design in Contemporary Culture. New York: Princeton Architectural Press, 1997.

Lupton, Elaine and Miller, J. Abbott, editors.
The ABCs of the Bauhaus and Design Theory. New York: Princeton Architectural Press, 1995.

McLean, Ruari.
Jan Tschichold: Typographer. London: Lund Humphries, 1975.

Meggs, Philip B.
A History of Graphic Design, Third Edition. New York: John Wiley & Sons, 1998.

Müller-Brockmann, Josef.
The Graphic Artist and His Design Problems. Teufen AR, Switzerland: Verlag Arthur Niggli, 1968.

Müller-Brockmann, Josef.
Grid Systems in Graphic Design. Niederteufen: Verlag Arthur Niggli, 1981.

Naylor, Gilliam.
The Bauhaus Reassessed: Sources and Design Theory. Herbert, 1985.

Purvis, Alston.
Dutch Graphic Design: 1918–1945. New York: Van Nostrand Reinhold, 1992.

Rand, Paul.
Thoughts on Design. New York: Van Nostrand Reinhold, 1970.

Rotzler, Willy.
Constructive Concepts. New York: Rizzoli, 1977.

Ruder, Emil.
Typography. Teufen AR, Switzerland: Arthur Niggli, 1968.

Tschichold, Jan.
Die Neue Typographie (The New Typography). Berlin: Verlag des Bildungsverbandes, 1928.

Tschichold, Jan.
Designing Books. New York: Wittenborn, Schultz, Inc., 1951.

Venturi, Robert; Brown, Denise Scott; Izenour, Steven.
Learning from Las Vegas. Cambridge, MA: MIT Press, 1977.

Weingart, Wolfgang.
My Way to Typography. Lars Müller Verlag: Baden, Switzerland, 2000.

About the Author Timothy Samara is a graphic designer and educator based in New York City, where he divides his time between teaching at the School of Visual Arts and the Fashion Institute of Technology, and writing and consulting through STIM Visual Communication. His design work focuses on identity development and information design for corporate and nonprofit clients, in projects spanning print, environmental, and digital media. He has taught and lectured at the University of the Arts, Philadelphia, Newhouse School of Communications, Syracuse University; Western Michigan University; Rensselaer Polytechnic Institute in Troy, New York; and SUNY Fredonia. He graduated a Trustee Scholar from the University of the Arts in 1990 with a BFA in graphic design. Tim lives in New York's Chelsea district with his partner of four years.

Acknowledgments

Assembling material for a book of this kind depends on the good will of so many busy people. My sincere thanks to all of the designers who collected examples of their work for consideration, for their suggestions, and for their great encouragement. In that regard I extend a special thanks to Hans Bockting, Katherine McCoy, and Simon Johnston, whose investment of time and helpful advice greatly exceeded my expectations. Thank you to Richard Wilde at the School of Visual Arts, who initially put Rockport Publishers in touch with me.

I am grateful to Massimo Vignelli, who unexpectedly and very graciously gave me four hours out of his busy day to meet with me and speak in-depth about this book's subject.

My thanks also to Chris Myers, at the University of the Arts in Philadelphia, and his partner, Nancy Mayer, who collected and organized a prodigious stack of student work to consider.

And last, but certainly not least, to Sean and Catherine, for their patience and support throughout the entire process.